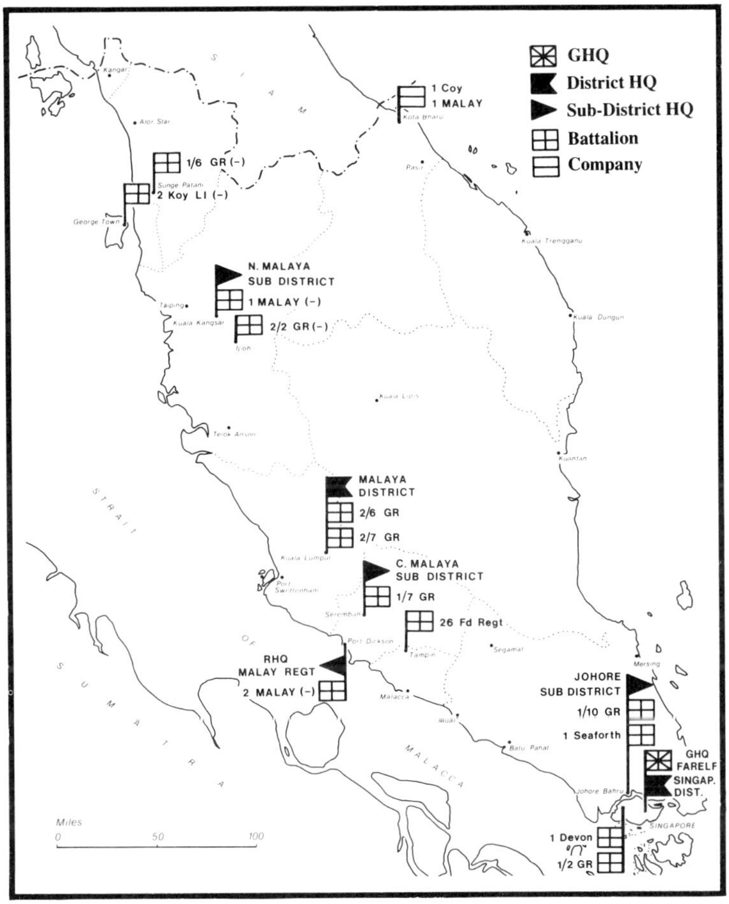

Right:

Locations of Army headquarters and units, 2 July 1948 (at the out break of the Malayan Emergency).

Below:

A watchtower manned by Malayan Home Guards in order to protect a railway bridge.
IWM

miners. In June of that year the police force had a tiny Special Branch, far too small for the task which faced its members at the beginning of the Emergency. Even worse, however, was the government's political machine — one that was outmoded and quite unable to cope with a war situation. In the face of this sudden insurrection, and at a time when urgent decisions were demanded, Malaya had 11 separate governments. Each of the nine smaller states had its own Sultan, assisted by a Malayan 'Prime Minister' and British Adviser. The administrations of two other territories, Penang and Malacca, were headed by British officers from the Malayan Civil Service. All the states were linked by the Federal Government in Kuala Lumpur and came under the authority of the British High Commissioner, Sir Edward Gent. As High Commissioner, Sir Edward Gent had an impressive record behind him, in peace and in war, winning a double first, and between 1939 and 1945 a DSO and MC. Since March 1946 his high-minded zeal for reform had caused him to be disliked by what he called the 'old brigade' — and the dislike was mutual. He had been warned by many of the British Advisers about Communist preparations the year before but unfortunately he had not taken heed. When the insurrection broke out and the killings multiplied, the High Commissioner found himself being forced by public opinion to introduce repressive measures that were badly needed to blunt the Communist offensive. However, such measures were often repugnant to Sir Edward's high ideals and soon he was to be attacked bitterly by the European planters for his reluctance to declare an all-out war against the terrorists.

Complacency was not confined to the civil administration and the police. Gen Sir Charles Boucher, the small, pugnacious Army commander, felt able to express his confidence in victory by telling the Press, 'I can tell you this is by far the easiest problem I have ever tackled. In spite of the appalling country, the enemy is far weaker in technique and courage than either the Greek or Indian Reds'. There is no evidence to show that anyone in authority disagreed with the General at the time (mid-June 1948) so that his assessment can be taken as a reflection of the views of the Special Branch and Military Intelligence.

The Commissioner-General for South-East Asia, Malcolm MacDonald, appreciated that all was not well at the top of the government in Malaya. When he received a report from a senior policeman which showed that the Communist Terrorist (CT) strength consisted of a minimum of 5,000 active fighters, supported by a quarter of a million of Min Yuen in the towns and villages, MacDonald went to see the High Commissioner who ridiculed the figures. After MacDonald had cabled his misgivings to London, Sir Edward Gent was recalled to the United Kingdom on 29 June. It was intended that he would be dismissed but Fate was not to allow him the chance even to defend his policies because he was killed in an aircraft crash on his way to London. His successor was Sir Henry Gurney who was destined to remain at the helm as High Commissioner until his death two years to the very day after taking up the appointment, a period that saw the darkest days of the Emergency.

To exacerbate the problem that faced the new High Commissioner, there was no overall 'Supremo' so that a lack of day-to-day co-operation between the Army, the police and the civil government resulted. This invariably meant that troops and police were rushed hither and thither in unsuccessful attempts to stave off attacks on isolated police posts, rubber estates or tin mines. On many occasions the Security Forces arrived too late, their sudden abortive dash being the result of rumours which were passed on to the local commander as being information of operational value. As a consequence the Security Forces were doomed to carry out a seemingly never-ending stream of pointless searches and patrols. The term 'jungle bashing' was heard more and more to describe days of sweat and frustration without any reward, and often without any signs that the terrorists had ever been near the particular stretch of jungle. The National Servicemen in the British units and the newly joined recruits serving in the Gurkha battalions all had to learn the hard way — as opposed to their adversaries, the majority of whom were experienced in the art of living and fighting in the jungle as a result of the years spent operating against the occupying Japanese between 1942 and 1945.

Leadership at all levels was of a varying standard in the police and Army. As time went by it was to improve when the less efficient were removed and the weaker commanders cracked or resigned voluntarily. In many respects the police faced bigger problems than the Army, with factions growing up as ex-Palestine police officers were posted in as part of the rapid expansion necessary to meet the threat. A troubled police force undoubtedly had repercussions throughout the country and this did not help to establish a happy relationship with the military officers who were now working alongside it.

The first task was a holding operation, keeping the CTs on the move by constant searching, patrolling and ambushing but it was to take some time before even these operations could be organised properly. The pressure was particularly heavy on the infantry battalions, most of whom had large contingents of untrained men, especially in the Gurkha units. Training Gurkha recruits has always been a lengthy, albeit well-ordered business, but

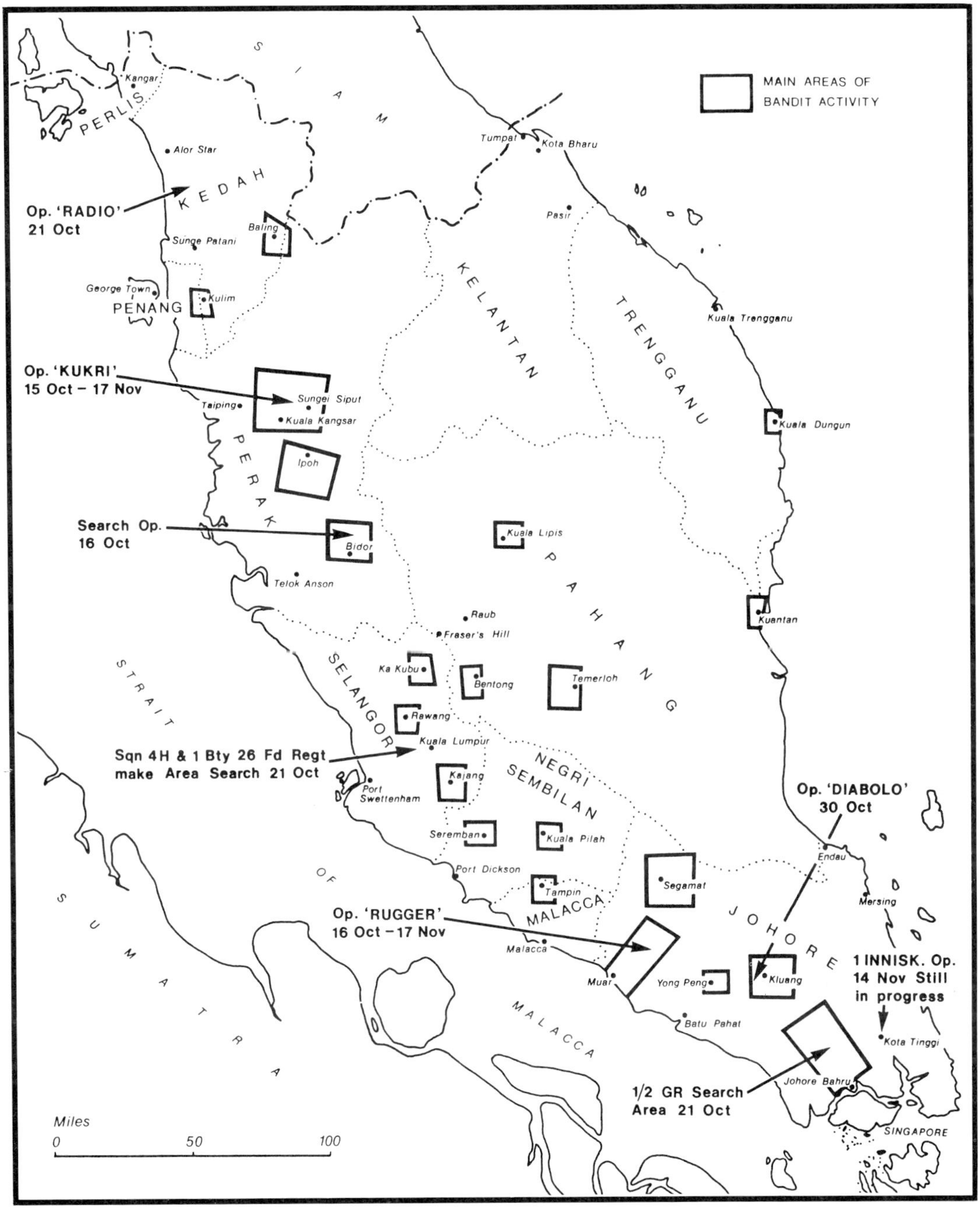

Above:
A busy time for both sides: principal areas of activity, 1 October to 19 November 1948.

The chain of command, Far East Land Forces (during 1950 until early 1951)

FAR EAST LAND FORCES
(Singapore)

- **Singapore Base District**
  - 1 Singapore Regt RA
    (less one Tp)
    (Trg Cadre only)
- **HQ Brit Forces Hong Kong**
  - **Land Forces Hong Kong**
    - *28 INF BDE*
      - 1 KOSB
      - 1 KSLI
      - 1 S Staffords
    - *UNBRIGADED*
      - One Sqn 4H
      - 3 R Tks
      - 14 Fd Regt
      - 23 Fd Regt
      - 25 Fd Regt (less one bty)
      - 58 Med Regt
      - 27 HAA Regt
      - 34 LAA Regt
      - 27 4.2 Mortar Bty (less det in Korea)
      - 120 4.2 Mortar Bty
      - 24 Fd Engr Regt
      - 67 Gurkha Fd Sqn
      - 68 Gurkha Fd Sqn
      - 1 R Leicesters
      - 1 Wilts
- **HQ Malaya**
  (Kuala Lumpur)
  - **HQ North Malaya Sub District**
    (Kamunting)
    - *HQ 3 CDO BDE RM*
      (Ipoh)
      - 4 H (less three Sqns)
      - 40 RM Cdo
      - 42 RM Cdo
      - 45 RM Cdo
    - *1 MALAY BDE*
      (Kota Bahru)
      - 3 Malay
    - *1 KOYLI*
  - *HQ 48 GURKHA INF BDE*
    (Kuala Lipis)
    - One Sqn 4 H
    - 1 Seaforth
    - 1/10 GR
    - 2/7 GR
    - 2 Malay
    - 4 Malay
  - **HQ South Malay District**
    (Seremban)
    - *HQ 18 INF BDE*
      (Kuala Lumpur)
      - One Sqn 13/18 H
      - 2 SG
      - 1 Suffolk
      - Malayan Engr Sqn
    - *HQ 26 GURKHA INF BDE*
      (Johore Bahru)
      - 13/18 HJ (less two Sqns)
      - One Tp 1 Singapore Regt RA
      - 1 Cameronians
      - 1 Worc R
      - 1/2 GR
      - 2/2 GR
      - 2/6 GR
      - 2/10 GR
    - *HQ 63 GURKHA INF BDE*
      (Seremban)
      - One Sqn 13/18 H
      - 26 Fd Regt RA
      - One Bty 25 Fd Regt RA
      - 1 Green Howards
      - 1/6 GR
      - 1/7 GR
      - 1 Malay

the alarms in Malaya during 1948 saw young half-trained soldiers being despatched to guard key points or on occasions being sent into the jungle on active service. On more than one occasion recruits who had not fired a shot were detailed to carry out operational guard duties; one report mentions that the order was given to them 'to refrain from loading their rifles but to use the kukri or bayonet instead'. There is little doubt that the almost complete disruption of training within the Brigade of Gurkhas was a handicap to the majority of the 1948 recruits for the rest of their service.

With few contacts and the spasmodic information from the terrorised locals being generally unreliable, operations usually consisted of sweeps designed to flush the CTs out into ambushes, or 'stops' (as they were known). Gradually these large scale operations, expensive in time and effort, were to be abandoned in favour of company or platoon patrols which were sent into a given area to carry out intensive tracking and searches over a specified period. It became a long and deadly game of hide and seek which was to mean literally hundreds of hours spent in hunting an elusive enemy, over many weary miles through rubber, jungle and swamp, often in heavy monsoon downpours, interspersed with long periods spent in mosquito-ridden ambush positions.

In the beginning the CTs tended to use large and well equipped camps in the jungle, which contained parade grounds, basket-ball pitches, lecture halls, as well as 'bashas'. In such a manner had they fought the Japanese, but as the British became better organised, air reconnaissance was used to pinpoint these camps, often conspicuous from the air, and after several setbacks the CTs learnt to operate in smaller parties which were based on better camouflaged camps, constructed to house less men and women in increasingly spartan conditions.

It was during this period towards the end of 1948 that the true significance of the squatter settlements was appreciated fully by both sides. Chin Peng's jungle fighters had begun to rely on their support, exploiting those who sympathised and intimidating those who preferred not to be involved in the struggle. In various parts of the country there were some 600,000 squatters and as long as they existed in their many groups, the Communist's Phase One stood every chance of being successful. For the jungle fighters food was no problem and although it was obvious that the squatter settlements were being used to store food stocks as well as offering a refuge for terrorists on the run, the Government still held its hand. In frustration, the military and police had to content themselves with making surprise raids which invariably led to the discovery and confiscation of large quantities of rice and other foodstuffs.

Nevertheless, contrary to Chin Peng's optimistic forecast, there was no wholesale evacuation of isolated rubber plantations, small towns or mining communities, so that, armed with hindsight, it can be said that the Communists never looked like achieving their ambitious Phase One. At the onset their military units were too large and unwieldy for the classical concept of guerilla warfare and, of equal importance, they did not win the local people over willingly to their cause; instead they pressed on with their strategy of all-out terrorism including a series of brutal murders. Moreover, the Security Forces had a stroke of luck, when within a month of the Emergency being declared, Chin Peng's most experienced military adviser, 34-year old Lau Yew, who had been a brilliant guerilla fighter when operating against the Japanese with Force 136, was killed by a police officer who was acting on chance information. The loss of Lau Yew was a crippling blow from which Chin Peng never really recovered for he had been the one Communist leader with any real pretentions to being a military tactician.

Although the weakness of Chin Peng's overall strategy during the first few months can be seen clearly now, at the time, and indeed for the next two years, the outlook for democracy in Malaya was grim. Despite the terrorists' first onslaught having been blunted by intensive military and police activity, the enemy was far from being defeated, although after being forced to withdraw deeper into the jungle the chances of them setting up secure 'liberated' bases diminished, thus nullifying the main aim of their Phase One. Nevertheless the CTs were still able to emerge from their jungle haunts in order to commit atrocities against 'running dogs' as well as innocent victims.

By the time Chin Peng called his second Party conference early in 1949, held once more in Pahang, his Communist followers had killed during the first six months 482 police, troops and civilians (including 24 British planters and miners), and had inflicted wounds on a further 404 people. Against this, their losses virtually balanced those of the British, with 406 CTs being killed and 268 captured. But behind those grim figures Chin Peng's grandiose dreams of hounding the British forces to defeat had gone away; there were as yet no liberated areas; the government under the new High Commissioner was getting tougher: in particular, there was Emergency Regulation 17D which granted it powers to uproot entire villages if there was evidence of support for Chin Peng's jungle fighters, and to take the villagers away into detention camps.

At the 1949 jungle conference, which was attended by several Chinese Red Army officers who had arrived by various means with the apparent aim of helping Chin Peng reorganise his

Above:

A bandit camp for about 100 found by a patrol of the 1 KOYLI. As the Emergency continued, the CTs used much smaller camps in order to avoid detection from the air. *IWM*

Right:

A patrol from 1 Cameronians with caps and flags captured after it had surprised a bandit camp. *IWM*

striking force, the name of the Communist Army was changed to 'Malayan Races' Liberation Army' (MRLA) in an attempt to enlist the support of the other races in Malaya — the Malays and Indians — into joining the predominantly Chinese organisation that existed at every level. Only in one state did Malays, serving the Party, comprise the bulk of the locally-based 10th Regiment which was commanded by a notorious bandit called Abdullah. It was at the same conference that Abdullah received orders from Chin Peng to begin a campaign in the essentially Malay state of Pahang. Still clinging to his dream of establishing a liberated area, Chin Peng ordered Abdullah to start an intensified recruiting drive among the kampong Malays and, by using terror if necessary, to build up an all-Malay Regiment.

Recruiting Malays to Communism was no easy task and by using 'killer squads' Abdullah ran the risk of turning his co-religionists against his cause. This did not deter him; he was a ruthless fighter and had already taken over and held an area around the railway town of Kuala Krau for five days, the only time in the Emergency that Chin Peng was to realise his concept of establishing a Communist-controlled liberated area. His attack on Kuala Krau resulted in the death of a British engineer, six Malay police and the derailment of an armoured train. Abdullah's brutal tactics meant that he was feared, but at the same time he forced many local people into declaring that they must organise themselves to withstand his thugs. As a result, the Sultan of Pahang nominated his Secretary, Yeop Mahidin, to lead the loyal Malays, in the knowledge that Yeop had fought with gallantry in the war as an officer in Force 136: of more importance, Yeop was a cousin of Abdullah, thus knowing how his mind worked and his likely tactics. From a small beginning and after selecting a personal bodyguard Yeop eventually raised the Pahang Kampong Guards, which by the time the Emergency ended numbered some 26,000. The vendetta between the cousins was a bitter one. Yeop set about his task with patience; he toured the kampongs, explaining to the villagers that the Government intended to grant independence as soon as the Emergency was over — and this would take a democratic form rather than a regime of terror which Abdullah and his supporters were trying to impose. Information of operational value began to flow in which led to Abdullah narrowly escaping death at the hands of Yeop; he was discredited and was forced to flee the country, never to return during the Emergency.

Throughout the country information was the key factor and just as long as the squatters were organised into their Min Yuen cells, the CTs would continue to pose a formidable threat to Malaya. Sir Henry Gurney decided to resettle all these Chinese people, giving them plots of land after re-grouping them into New Villages in which they could be protected and isolated from the Communists. This ambitious scheme was subsequently known as the Briggs Plan. Such a momentous decision set in motion months of detailed and intricate planning so that it was to take a long time before the implications of such a scheme were understood by Chin Peng and his comrades. The plan was called after the new Director of Operations, Lt-Gen Sir Harold Briggs who, after retiring from the Army, was asked to come back as the Chief Executive to the High Commissioner, to be Director of Operations with full authority over all the Security Forces but subject, of course, to Sir Henry Gurney in major matters of policy. Briggs was one of the main architects of this, the long-term plan which was to play such a major part in the counter-offensive against the Communist guerillas of Malaya.

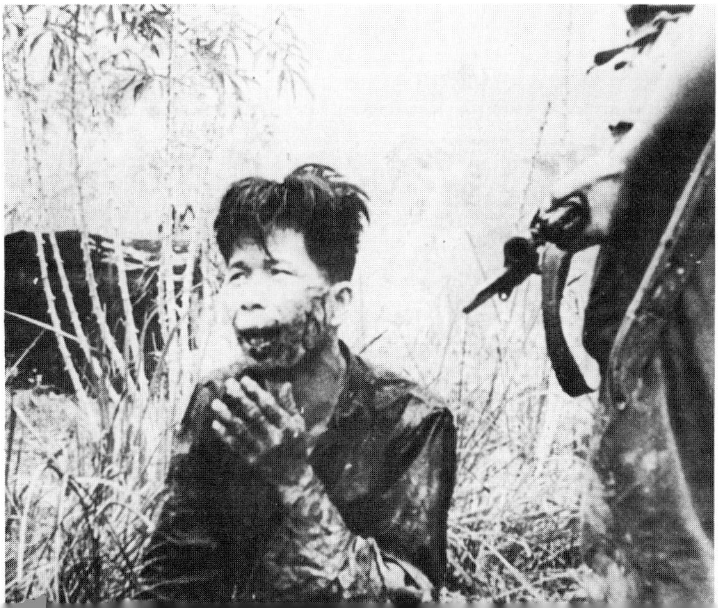

Left:
A wounded terrorist after being captured in 1950. Following good treatment, many of these helped the Security Forces in future operations. *IWM*

2 The Counter-Strategy

From the end of 1949 until the end of 1951 both sides thought the other was winning, thus emphasising one of the ironies of war when the power of the enemy becomes magnified out of all proportion. During those three years, Chin Peng's elusive CTs had been able to pick the time and place of any battle before disappearing into the obscurity of the jungle and, in the eyes of the Security Forces, had taken on almost superhuman qualities. But at the height of the killings, Chin Peng was to call yet another meeting of his Politburo in late October 1951 at which he reviewed their successes and failures and, in a dramatic reversal and admission, announced completely new tactics — when neither side looked like winning although each thought the other was on the verge of a victory.

Before we consider the British long term strategy which was to turn the tide from imminent defeat into victory, let us listen in on Chin Peng as he admitted that his initial campaign had misfired; the campaign of terrorism with which the Party had hoped to win the support of the population and force the British to abandon Malaya to the Communists. In an extraordinarily honest assessment, the Secretary General confessed that the Party had acted on a totally false premise — the terror tactics which had worked against the Japanese had not produced the same dramatic results against the 'British Colonialists'. The people were weary of living in constant fear and the policy of slashing rubber trees and damaging machinery had turned them against the Communists, particularly when they saw their daily rice ration cut and their livelihood taken away from them. Now, belatedly in October 1951, all unnecessary 'inconvenience' was to be avoided: no longer were there to be burnings of New Villages or attacks on public services, no longer were the coolies' ration cards to be seized and burnt. The attacks against troops and police were, of course, to continue but in other directions peaceful overtures were to be the order of the day; Trade Unions were to be penetrated and the masses influenced by the Min Yuen rather than by terrorising them with thoughts of death or torture. In short, Chin Peng, for the first time, accepted Mao Tse Tung's classic principle of a struggle on two equal fronts: the war of terrorism against the police and troops on the one hand combined with legal infiltration into important parts of society on the other.

Chin Peng's dream of seizing towns or large villages and setting up liberated areas had been dropped but he was still confident that his fighting force would triumph in the end, especially when Communism was thriving in China and the Red Army volunteers had intervened to such good effect in the Korean war. By keeping the armed struggle going against the British, he hoped that they would tire of the protracted war and leave their colonial possession of Malaya to the tender mercy of the MCP. In effect Chin Peng had changed from his short-term plan which so nearly succeeded to a long-term one at the same time as the plans drawn up by Sir Henry Gurney and his advisers back in 1949 were coming to fruition. Tragically Sir Henry Gurney did not live to see this happen because he was killed in a road ambush by the CTs in October 1951, an event that shocked the nation. Belatedly the British Government in London appreciated that the Emergency would be lost if something drastic was not done and done quickly. The unplanned assassination by the CTs of Sir Henry Gurney not only marked the blackest day in the Emergency but also proved to be the event that spurred everyone into action, even if it was to take many more years of toil before the outcome was assured. No longer could the British Government delay the appointment of a Supremo, the man who would combine the duties of High Commissioner and Director of Operations.

During his two-year tenure as High Commissioner, Gurney had insisted that the Government should rule and not declare martial law, maintaining that it was a war of conflicting ideologies which meant armed support for the political struggle rather than the other way around. One of Gurney's chief advisers, a man who was to continue to give equally valuable counsel to his successor, was Robert (later Sir Robert) Thompson. He argued: 'It's all very well having bombers, masses of

Left:
Communist Terrorists slashed rubber trees as part of their campaign against the Malayan economy. *IWM*

Below:
Villagers load their possessions on to trucks prior to their move to a New Village in 1952. *IWM*

Bottom:
Once resettled in a New Village, the Chinese are guarded against any CT attack, as well as being under the watchful eye of the Security Forces. *IWM*

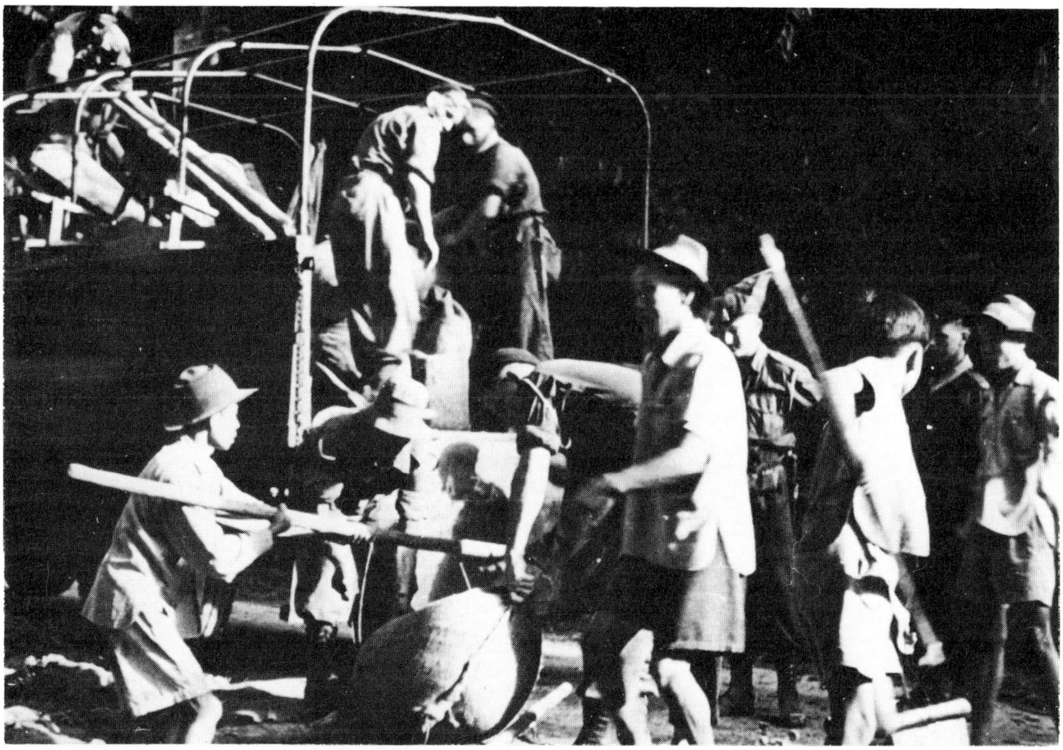

helicopters, tremendous firepower, but none of these will eliminate a Communist cell in a High School which is producing 50 recruits a year for the insurgent movement'.

It was an argument that was to be of vital importance especially when the world was to see the opposite viewpoint being taken by the United States of America during its participation in the long and tragic struggle in Vietnam. The maxim that it is better to police villages than to destroy them, that one stray bomb killing one innocent child can make a thousand enemies, was always in the minds of the British leaders in Malaya. As a consequence the Royal Air Force rarely bombed or 'straffed' targets near any town or populated area throughout the Emergency. Its vital contribution lay in other fields: in air reconnaissance; in the air dropping of supplies to the numerous units and sub-units, Army and Police Field Force operating in the jungles; in casualty evacuation; and in providing much needed mobility for the Security Forces with RN and RAF helicopters being used to move troops from one point to another when searching out and subsequently attacking suspected Communist camps.

As stated before, Sir Henry Gurney's most historic contribution to victory was when he took the momentous decision to uproot and resettle the 600,000 Chinese squatters who had been living on the fringes of the jungle on land to which they had no real title or right. Ironically, such a social revolution might never have been attempted had it not been for the Emergency. During the planning stages one of the biggest problems was secrecy before specific orders were given for groups of squatters to be uprooted from selected areas and removed in Army transport to one of the many New Villages, ready to house them. Here, the Communist propagandists proclaimed, the villagers would be prisoners behind wire fences and perimeter lighting, with everyone being given a number and registered in the office of the Resettlement Officer. Each of these allegations contained a grain of truth but at the same time the squatters were protected and, for the first time since their forbears settled in Malaya, they were able to build their own houses and farm land that was to be theirs in the eyes of the law.

Full-scale resettlement began in earnest during 1949 and by the end of 1951 more than two-thirds of the squatters were living in 509 New Villages. Chin Peng fought hard to gain control of these villages and it was to be many months before the Briggs Plan began to bear fruit. Its authors had advocated that the Security Forces should protect the populated areas, isolate the terrorists in their camps from the New Villages and, by cutting off their food supplies, force the jungle fighters out into the open, to walk into the ambushes mounted by the Army and police. It was an operation which was run by the Government in conjunction with the Security Forces — in contrast to Vietnam where the Government was run by a military junta, so often dissociated from the civilians in what should have been a joint struggle against the common foe.

Before his death, Sir Henry Gurney made two more far-reaching decisions. The first was to announce a system of rewards for information leading to the killing or capture of CTs — with Chin Peng being worth $80,000 at the top of the list. The real hope behind the plan was to persuade surrendered CTs to sell their erstwhile comrades for cash bounties, and though many in the UK deplored the move on moral grounds, in the end it proved to be one of the biggest war-winning weapons. Surrendered CTs were offered a half-rate of the standard reward and many of them persuaded others to give up the struggle, thus earning enough money to set themselves up in business thereafter.

The second major decision angered Chin Peng more than any other taken by the High Commissioner: National Registration cards were issued to all civilians in Malaya. Every man, woman or child over the age of 12 had to possess an identity card bearing a thumb print and photograph. This plan was bitterly assailed in the left-wing press with the Communists being always ready to fan the fears expressed by the many people. Their propaganda line was, 'It will be a prelude to conscription so do not register , instead lose your card, or hand it over to us, we will burnt it'. Thereafter civilian buses were stopped and tappers were contacted on labour estates for the CTs to take the identity cards which they ceremoniously burnt before the owners' eyes as a gesture of contempt. These registration cards gave invaluable help to the Security Forces because they were able to separate the sheep from the goats: if a man was questioned and he could not produce a card, then he was immediately suspect. Chin Peng was forced to institute another campaign of terror with one objective in mind: wrecking Gurney's National Registration plan. Government registration teams visiting remote villages were attacked while photographers engaged by the Government were murdered by anti-registration squads of CTs specially formed to operate in various parts of the country. These were the months of the killings which shocked thousands of civilians who had been sitting on the fence, waiting to see which way the wind would blow.

But by the middle of 1951, with two-thirds of the squatters already settled, the Government's measures were beginning to work, and despite the crude bouts of violence by the CTs, the Chinese in the New Villages were settling down gradually to

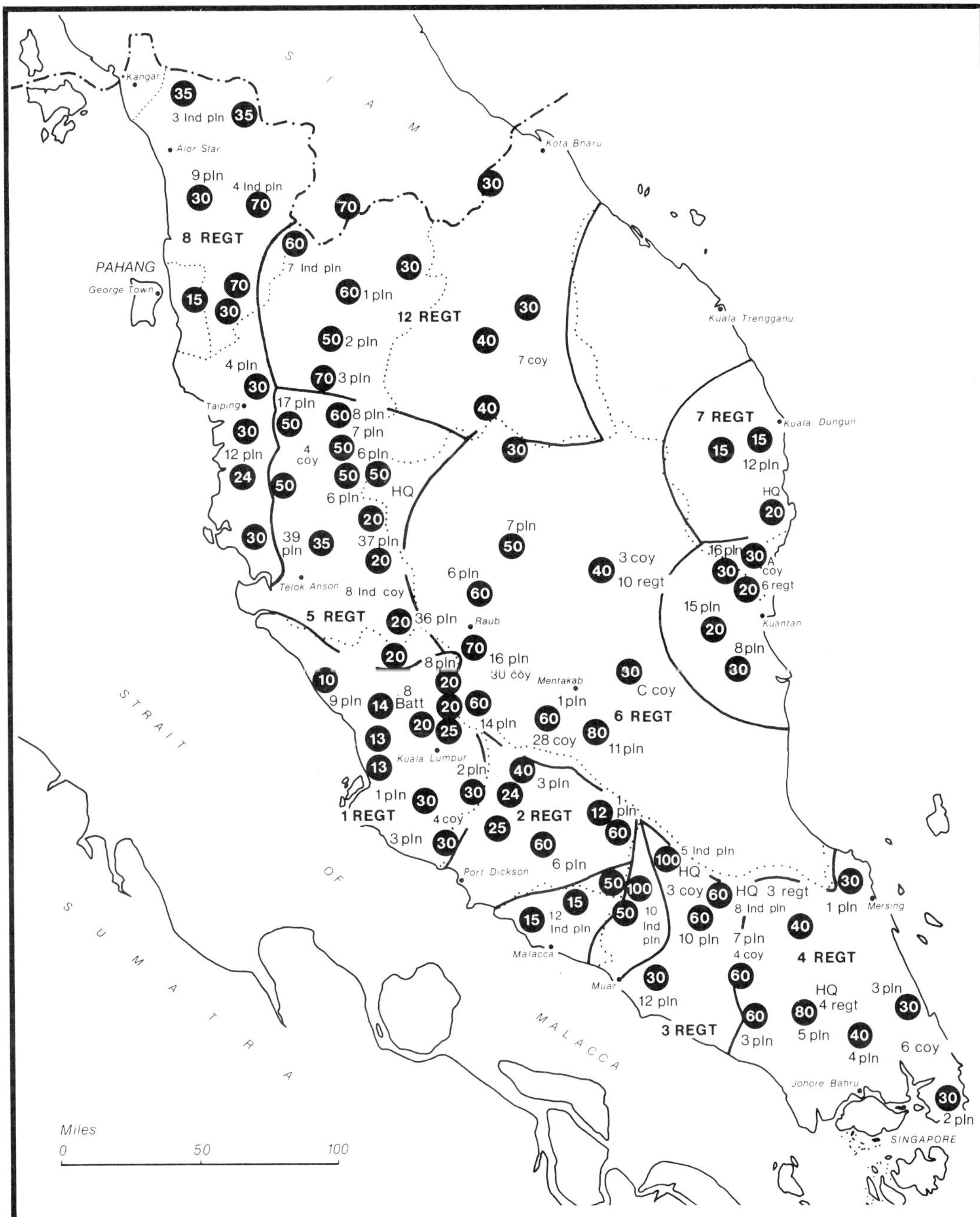

Above:
Malayan Races Liberation Army dispositions, August 1951.

Left:
As part of the Government's campaign to resettle all illegal squatters, a site is cleared for a Chinese New Village in 1952. *IWM*

Malayan Races Liberation Army (MRLA) — Chain of Command

- GHQ (Central Committee MCP)
  - HQ Northern Zone (N Malayan Bureau MCP)
    - (State Committees MCP)
      - HQ No 12 Regiment (N Perak/ N Kelantan) — *Strength* 460
      - HQ No 8 Regiment (Kedah/ Perlis) — *Strength* 270
      - HQ No 5 Regiment (Perak/ W Kelantan) — *Strength* 550
  - HQ Central Zone (Cen Malaya Bureau MCP)
    - (State Committees MCP)
      - HQ No 6 Regiment (W Pahang) — *Strength* 380
      - HQ No 10 Regiment (Malaya) (Central Pahang) — *Strength* 100
      - HQ No 7 Regiment (S Trengganu) — *Strength* 150
      - HQ No 1 Regiment (Selangor) — *Strength* 220
      - HQ No 2 Regiment (Negri Sembilan) — *Strength* 250
  - HQ Southern Zone (S Malaya Bureau MCP)
    - (State Committees MCP)
      - HQ No 3 Regiment (N Johore/ Malacca) — *Strength* 250
      - HQ No 9 Regiment (C Johore) — *Strength* 280
      - HQ No 4 Regiment (S Johore) — *Strength* 370

Note: This Order of Battle includes only formations from GHQ level down to regiment level. The larger regiments were divided into military sub-districts, battalions or companies, while the smaller regiments were divided into platoons. The strength of individual units at the same level varied considerably. Approximate strengths of regiments shown above were for the period January to August 1951.

their very different existence. Resettlement officers toured their areas urging the Chinese to use their votes to select the village's own councillors, who, after being elected, would run the community's affairs. Not surprisingly, few stepped forward to volunteer at the beginning because they were terrified that such a gesture would lead them into being marked as anti-Communist, facing certain death as soon as they left the village and its protection. Slowly, very slowly, the more responsible Chinese were won over but for a considerable time food was still smuggled out of many New Villages, together with medicines and other materials that would be useful for the jungle-based CTs. To counter this a sweeping list of restricted goods, ranging from rice to paper and printing materials, was drawn up by the Government, and it became a major task for the Army, as well as the police, to man check points outside the villages, searching men, women and children as they left in the early hours of the morning to work on rubber estates or elsewhere. It was to become a game of hide and seek, a contest waged without humour and with the strictest of punishments whenever food or supplies were found in the illegal possession of any civilian. Not surprisingly searchers and searched became extremely proficient with the Chinese showing remarkable ingenuity in hiding their rice and grain in the most extraordinary places, while the searchers developed ideas on how to detect those who were attempting to run the gauntlet. It was tiring work and it needed a fund of tact and patience, otherwise many innocent people might have been mishandled and turned against the Government by unnecessarily thoughtless behaviour on the part of an individual soldier or policeman. Already the Government was realising that the battle would be won if the people were on their side rather than forcing them to co-operate against their will.

As a direct consequence of some of the New Villages being isolated from the CTs, Chin Peng's men had to establish different lines of communication and find alternative means of resupply if they were going to survive. This meant that more and more units or sub-units of the MRLA had to move which, in the long term, meant a victory for the Security Forces. As this pattern increased, the CTs were forced to retreat further and further into the deep jungle where they hoped they could obtain much-needed food and vegetables from the jungle people, the aborigines, or alternatively they themselves could grow their own vegetables after cutting down trees and cultivating strips as gardens. There was nothing dramatic about the move away from certain New Villages into the more isolated parts of the jungle, so that it was to take a considerable time before the changing pattern was recognised by Government Intelligence agencies. Survival for the CTs was still possible provided that their jungle 'gardens' were not located from the air which could lead to the subsequent destruction by ground troops. Bombing such targets was tried but proved to be pretty ineffective: the soft earth, thick vegetation and giant trees all combined to nullify blast damage to the minimum — as foot patrols were to report on many occasions when sent to investigate.

The increasing use of light reconnaissance aircraft, supported by Royal Navy and RAF helicopters, meant that it was only a question of time before those deep and isolated hiding places were dealt with by the Security Forces.

Although Chin Peng was still commanding a fighting force, the Communist directive of October 1951 was an important admission of partial defeat, a document that was to change the course of the long Emergency yet again. Unfortunately for the British, it was to take nearly 12 months before the first copy of the directive fell into the hands of the Special Branch so that, at a time when minds were numbed by the shock of hearing about the High Commissioner's death, morale in Malaya continued to plummet. Nevertheless, his murder made everyone realise that the insurrection's strength had been consistently underestimated: while Sir Henry Gurney's death was the low-water mark of the Emergency in Malaya it was also to mark the turning point of the conflict.

3 Templer at the Helm

Gen Sir Gerald Templer arrived at Kuala Lumpar in February 1952. He was an unconventional soldier with immense energy, a man who could use with effect a flow of withering language when he was upset by inefficiency or complacency: he made an immediate impact on everyone. Old-time colonial attitudes were anathema to him and his brusque manner hid the fact that he had the agile brain of a shrewd statesman. He had no time for artificial diplomacy and soon made it clear to his advisers that the days of the old colonial regime in Malaya were numbered. And to achieve this he was armed with more powers than any British soldier since Oliver Cromwell.

In a short time this man of drive and resolution had made it known that not only was he going to defeat the Communists but also he had been sent to prepare the country for complete independence. In his first circular to the Malayan Government, he was to write that 'any idea that the business of normal Civil Government and the business of the Emergency are two separate entities must be killed for good and all. The two activities are completely and utterly related'. For him there was no colour bar, while British, Rhodesians, Gurkhas, Africans and Fijians were risking their lives side by side with Malays, Chinese and Indians. Although he did not change his predecessor's policy or indeed Gurney's long-term strategy, Templer never forgot that his basic role was to prepare the country for self-government and he had a deep convinction that Malaya's independence could only succeed if the three main races were united. To this end he gave support to the leader of the United Malay National Organisation (UMNO), Tunku Abdul Rahman, who was later to form an alliance with the Malayan Chinese Association (MCA). That was a significant moment because Templer had recognised the Tunku as a man with whom he or his successor would have to negotiate.

Although Templer's initiatives in the political field were of long term importance, his first task was to stop the rot, to hold firm and raise the morale of the country, and thereafter win the military war. The sometimes peppery General realised that if the Emergency was going to be won, it would have to be a combined effort by the Army, the police and the civil administration.

The Combined Operations room at Kuala Lumpur was to be mirrored in every state and district throughout the country with State War Emergency Committees (SWEC) and District War Emergency Committees (DWEC) meeting regularly with the senior District Officer, police officer and Army commander preparing a joint plan at every level of government. Inevitably, some of the discussions were lengthy and not of direct interest to one or other of the triumvirate: there was often good reason for the sarcastic comment, 'war by committee is a waste of time'. Nevertheless, the principle was correct because it meant that the Security Forces could not act in an arbitrary manner nor could they carry out any operation which might affect the civilian population without clearing the matter first with the District Officer of the area.

Templer appreciated that the majority of the Chinese population in Malaya had been sitting on the fence and that they would have to be drawn into the struggle before the Government could claim that the nation, as a whole, was on its side. Like Gurney before him, he learnt to rely on Robert Thompson who had worked his way up from Chinese Affairs Officer until eventually he became Permanent Secretary of Defence. Robert Thompson, after the Emergency was over, was to be asked by President Nixon to visit Vietnam as adviser to the American Government. Unfortunately much of his advice was not accepted by the Americans, especially the senior military commanders: Thompson was a fervent believer that Communism could never be beaten by force of arms alone, but only by showing the people a better way of life. At Templer's side, Robert Thompson produced several ideas which were to be of supreme importance in winning over the Chinese. His deep understanding of that race led him into proposing that the Chinese Home Guards should be armed so that they could defend their New Villages and thus play an important part in the struggle against Communism. It was a gamble because there were many of Thompson's colleagues who affirmed that the Home Guards would hand the recently acquired weapons over to their friends or relatives, operating in the jungle. In one or two instances this did happen but in the long term, the Government's trust in the newly-raised Home Guards was to result in the men taking a firmer stand against the terrorists.

From the moment that Templer took over as 'Supremo', the Malayan people were to hear again and again that the war could only be won if their hearts and minds were won over to the Government's side. For the High Commissioner it meant a heavy programme of visits to schools, hospitals and institutions as well as receiving numerous delegations: at the same time, Lady Templer worked long hours starting womens' clubs and societies, opening new Red Cross branches and Community Centres: it was she who brought the Asian women into direct involvement with communal affairs for the first time in Malaya.

Now that the Army units had become more proficient in their jungle skills, Templer realised that the time had come for the police to play a far more crucial role because he was looking ahead to the day when the military would be very much in support. The police force had been expanded so that its Commissioner, Col Arthur Young, had responsibility for over a quarter of a million men, which included the Home Guard and Auxiliaries. The dramatic expansion had brought many problems particularly in the training of the newly-enlisted recruits. It was Templer who decided to second a number of Army majors to the Malayan police to act as training officers, a measure which did not please some of them, but the results justified the move. He also supported Young's request that the police should be given armoured cars, scout cars and a huge arsenal of guns and weapons: all this meant that during the following year the Police Commissioner was given £30,000,000 to be spent on the Malayan police, thus enabling him to transform them into an efficiently organised paramilitary force.

But perhaps one of the most important aspects Templer brought to the campaign was his emphasis on Intelligence. After World War 2 he had been Director of Military Intelligence in the War Office and this experience had a direct bearing on his attitude to the Emergency in Malaya for he thought in terms of Intelligence and the Special Branch. To this end he was to state that: 'Malaya is an Intelligence war, you can never beat Communism with troops alone'. He had appreciated that a large proportion of the Army and police operations had been abortive because they had been based on insufficient or inaccurate information — or both. By building up the Special Branch, and ensuring that it had far better liaison with Army Intelligence, gradually — and it was gradually — the flow of information about the CTs, their supporters in the Min Yuen and their all-important food supplies, started to come in, and successes achieved by the Security Forces became more frequent.

Inevitably there were setbacks, whereupon Templer himself would set off to see what had happened. Near the town of Tanjong Malim, the CTs ambushed and killed the District Officer, Public Works Engineer and seven policemen. Three days later, Templer, burning with a cold fury, descended on the township. He summoned 350 community leaders to meet him, and speaking with a savage anger he accused them of helping the CTs. For an hour he lectured them before announcing a collective punishment for 'the crime of silence'. There was to be a 22-hour a day curfew on the town, people would only be allowed to leave their homes between noon and 2pm. No one was to leave the town: schools would be closed, buses would cease to run, the rice ration would be halved. In return, he arranged for a letter and question form to be delivered to every household in Tanjong Malim. Every form had to be returned whether it contained information or not and Templer promised no one but he would see the contents.

Not surprisingly, this collective punishment produced a storm in Britain with some of the left-wing press describing it as odious and lamentable. But Templer had no time to be concerned about opinions expressed in Whitehall or Fleet Street and as a result of the information obtained by this means, 38 arrests were made. On that day, the day of the arrests, the curfew was lifted and there followed a new surge of spirit which astonished everyone — even Templer. Within days the locally-based guerilla platoon had realised there would be no more assistance from the townspeople. Within weeks, some 3,500 men from a district with one of the worst records in the war, volunteered to join the Home Guard; Tanjong Malim was to be one of the most peaceful areas in the whole of Malaya thereafter.

The tide was now turning in Malaya as month by month the number of Communist Terrorist incidents dropped. Templer's priorities had much to do with this for he never forgot that it was a civilian war. He was showing the greatest percipience in the field of politics by not only galvanising a lumbering administration but improving relations within the various branches of the Government. He avoided moving too slowly and, unlike some of the professional diplomats elsewhere in the dwindling British Empire, he avoided backing a loser in the independence stakes: he put his trust in the

Tunku and his trust was to be repaid. The huge resettlement plan with New Villages being set up all over the country meant that area after area was being taken from the Communists' control as the villagers' determination to defend their homes and families increased as they saw that the Government was winning. Now, in the far-off jungle bases, the mounting Communist Terrorist losses caused their leader, Chin Peng, to make yet another far-reaching decision in 1953. He announced that he and a small group of dedicated henchmen would flee from Malaya and direct the war from a jungle base just over the border with Thailand. It was an admission of defeat, even if by doing so it ensured that he and his own hard core of supporters would escape death or captivity like the rest of the MRLA which was being left to carry on the struggle. It says much for the guerillas' dedication and loyalty that they were prepared to risk all while their leader lived in comparative comfort — and safety — in his Thai sanctuary, accompanied by a 'staff' of 80 men.

One of the subordinates who eventually surrendered was to say that when Chin Peng made the announcement at this, his last conference on Malayan soil: 'The faces around me were incredulous. We had spent nearly five years in the jungle but this was such terrible news that for the first time it crossed my mind that perhaps we were going to lose the war'.

Left:
The Director of Operations and High Commissioner, Gen Sir Gerald Templer, inspects Fijian soldiers. The Fijians proved themselves to be formidable jungle fighters. *IWM*

Below left:
A Leading Scout of a King's African Rifles patrol in dense jungle. *IWM*

4 Security Forces — Tactics

With the tide now running strongly in favour of the British and the future independent nation of Malaya, let us now examine the tactics adopted by the Security Forces. The main lesson to be learned from counter-insurgency operations is that those waging a guerilla-type war can tie up lavishly-equipped modern regular forces 10 times their number in strength. Moscow and Peking have never underestimated their guerilla power. Thus it was at the start of the Emergency that the comparatively small number of terrorists had the Army and police units running round in circles, often to no avail. At the beginning the British had forgotten most of the jungle warfare techniques and expertise learned the hard way and at such high cost in the Burma campaign. Gradually the Gurkha units who served almost permanently in Malaya throughout the Emergency, and the British units, many of them containing large numbers of National Servicemen, after carrying out intensive jungle warfare courses, learned to do it better in the jungle than the Terrorists themselves. They were able to out-guerilla the enemy in every department, through sheer hard training and tremendous self-discipline, based on operational experience. In the main it was a platoon and section commanders' war, nevertheless it was the company commander who had to be able to set the example and do everything that his men could do, do it better and do it for longer.

Unlike the American policy in Vietnam of 'search and destroy' and then return to base, the British, Commonwealth and Gurkha soldiers in Malaya played the terrorist at his own game, by living out in the jungle for weeks on end and by winning the hearts and minds of the people they met until the jungle belonged to them. What then was the technique of domination of the jungle?

It was the ambush which was at one and the same time the guerillas' and the Security Forces' most potent weapon. Whether on a small or large scale, it was the key element. An ambush is merely another word for fighting from ground of one's own choosing — but with the difference that it depends entirely on complete surprise. An ambush in Malaya required all the tricks of the soldier's trade: an eye for country, track discipline, concealment, camouflage, silence, altertness, fire discipline, marksmanship, guile, cunning and, above all, self-discipline. It required constant training and rehearsal.

The type of fighting, the type of country and the climate called for individual stamina and fortitude, stout legs and hearts, agile brains and the acceptance of conditions in jungle and swamp, almost unimaginable in their demands on human endurance. Unlike the Americans in Vietnam, the helicopters were used not to strafe villages or populated areas, but to lift troops into the jungle either to positions from where they could attack likely Communist bases or to occupy 'stops', in ambush. As time passed, the large-scale sweeps and operations, controlled at brigade headquarters level, were used less and less. Tracking the small, quick-moving Communist Terrorist groups depended on accurate information, on expert and patient patrolling, while the actual contact often depended on luck, with the enemy presenting a fleeting target before disappearing at speed. Although the CTs reverted to a defensive role — as opposed to the first year or two when actions by 200-300 Communists were commonplace — they still retained the ability to hit back at unwary police or Army patrols or the occasional unescorted vehicle moving along roads ideally suited for ambushes.

While there was irrefutable proof that 'bandit hunting' was most effectively carried out under the direction of company commanders, working in districts that they and their men knew well, nevertheless for politico-military reasons large-scale operations for specific purposes were launched. An example from the regimental history of the 7th Gurkha Rifles is quoted below:

'Op "Hive" was designed to saturate a selected area of troops so that the terrorists' mode of life would be completely disrupted. A concentrated programme of police checks on roads and New Villages was planned in detail with the aim of

Above:
Specialised jungle equipment used by the Security Forces during the long Emergency in Malaya. *IWM*

Right:
'B' Squadron 22 SAS in a Beverley, prior to parachuting into the jungle. *IWM*

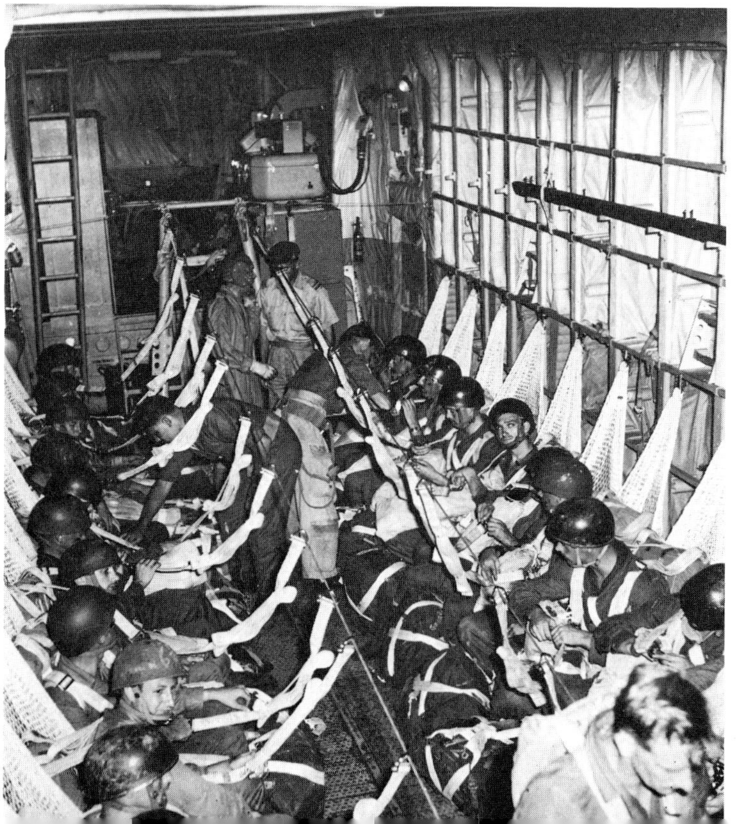

Above left:
Maj J. Douglas SAS, ready to parachute into the jungle, with a rope which will enable him to climb down from whichever tree he lands in. *IWM*

Above:
Recovering much-needed supplies dropped by parachute. *IWM*

Left:
A small jungle clearing used by SAS parachutists for operations against the CTs. *IWM*

driving the CTs back on to their jungle food dumps where they would be forced to eat up valuable reserves. Then the military units would move in to specific areas where it was hoped, by intensive ambushes and patrols, to force out the terrorists once more into the open or into the many "stop" (ambush) positions, established on recorded and likely tracks in the jungle surrounding Seremban . . .

'A lot of men were required to close the chinks in the jungle, many more than were available . . . To search for about 100 bandits, hiding in an area exceeding 600 square miles . . . only one sixteenth of the enemy were killed and in the opinion of one or two officers, not all this total was directly attributable to "Hive".'

The impatience of the troops was understandable but by now they were learning that there were no soft targets in the deep jungle. Each and every contact with the CTs was analysed, and it was estimated that an average soldier could be on patrol for 1,800 man hours before he could expect a contact with the enemy: contact having been made, the kill ratio was even more daunting as shooting at fleeing men in the jungle required marksmanship of a very high order.

While it could be said that it was an infantryman's war, supported in full measure by the police — especially when it was fought in and around rubber estates, tin mines and outside the wire fences of the New Villages — the soldiers had to rely far more on the Royal Air Force, and the Royal Naval and RAF helicopters, when they turned their attention to the CTs who had moved back into the deep jungle. Gradually it became clear that thousands of aborigines were being coerced by the Communists to grow food for them and to act as guides and mobile listening posts.

Initially the Government tried to induce the aborigines to leave their jungle homes and settle nearer villages and towns but, unused to civilisation, the 'Abos' contracted diseases and many literally pined to death, so it was decided to send them back to their homes in the jungle outback. The problem was how to keep in contact with them and at the same time prevent the CTs from bullying them into becoming subservient once more.

Gen Templer decided that to do this effectively required strategically placed jungle forts in the 'Abos' tribal grounds: based on these jungle forts, British and other troops serving alongside them in the Emergency would be able to remain for long periods in remote areas; eventually it was hoped that the police could take over and remain there permanently, acting as advance Intelligence posts as well as setting up small medical centres as part of the 'hearts and minds' campaign. Although there were initial setbacks in this ambitious scheme, and it was to take some time before there were any successes, gradually the 'Abos' were won over to the Government side with the result that a trickle of starving CTs started coming in to one or other of the forts in order to surrender. The helicopters and STOL Pioneers and Twin Pioneers had a big role to play in setting up the forts and restocking them thereafter, particularly as in some cases resupply by land would have taken several days.

From 1953 onwards more and more jungle plots and cultivations were being spotted by Army and RAF light aircraft. Vegetables planted in these gardens required sunlight for their growth and this entailed the felling of a number of trees. Once spotted, these cultivations were plotted on maps in the appropriate operations room, although it was quite another thing to deal effectively with them and their gardeners, who usually lived in a small lean-to nearby. Troops sent to destroy CT vegetable gardens often had to walk for days and invariably this meant taking at least one air drop during the approach march when the sight or sound of heavy aircraft was enough to alert the CTs, with the result that the patrols invariably found empty camps and could only relieve their feelings by wreaking their vengeance on the vegetables planted in neat rows by the conscientious Chinese 'gardener'. Crop spraying was tried by using chemical spray delivered by helicopters but it was only partially successful and the practice was abandoned later in the campaign.

The arrival of helicopters in larger numbers in Malaya changed matters dramatically and they were used for a multitude of purposes; in the search phase; in moving 'stops' once the CTs had been encountered; in bringing out dead or captured CTs and documents which were urgently required by Special Branch; and in evacuating sick and wounded members of the ground patrols. While it is true that the noise of the approaching helicopters undoubtedly warned the vigilant CTs, the psychological effect of noisy machines on men who had been hiding in the jungle for five or six years, constantly being hunted and harried, was a weapon that lowered morale appreciably.

Another successful measure from the air was the use of the Voice Aircraft, flying low over the jungle with a series of recorded messages aimed at CT waverers. From the air the CTs would hear messages telling them that certain of their leaders had surrendered or learn that rewards were being offered for information about their Regional Committees. By now the psychological importance of inducing terrorists to surrender was appreciated fully by both sides: indeed, the rate of surrenders slowly accelerated when the Government's ideas and methods of psychological warfare became

Above:
One of the jungle forts, Fort Sheen, set up to protect Aborigines from the CTs. *MoD*

Below left:
A Senoi guard at Fort Kemar. Once the Government had won their confidence the Aborigines were only too keen to help. *IWM*

Below:
An Aborigine assists the Security Forces. Their knowledge of rivers and tracks was of inestimable value. *IWM*

more and more effective. The desire to surrender was not always easy to put into effect as the CTs watched each other with suspicion and dealt with any deviationist trends ruthlessly. Some who wanted to surrender were caught and murdered in cold blood; others husbanded dreams in their hearts only to find no opportunity to escape because they were too afraid to take the risk. Several cases occurred when a terrorist surrendered himself, but only after being forced to kill a comrade who still wished to remain true to the Communist cause.

From 1954 onwards the Communist Terrorists were being forced to concentrate in certain identifiable areas of jungle wilderness. At such a time came directives inviting junior commanders to ask for the Royal Air Force to be used in an offensive role, with concentrated bombing on suspected camps in the jungle by Lincolns. The overall results did not justify such a generous use of air power which was as likely to kill innocent aborigines as Communist guerillas, and not surprisingly the infantry patrols regarded many of these sorties as being counter-productive. As a rule, air strikes were most effective when used in a supporting role during a particular operation, either to induce the CTs to move towards pre-positioned 'stops' or, if they had escaped the net, to make their journey thereafter more hazardous. This aspect is examined in more detail in Chapter 6.

If members of the bomber and fighter squadrons occasionally felt that their role in Malaya was unglamorous and barely appreciated, and that their potential was not used to the full, the air supply squadrons were worked to the bone because countless patrols, in various parts of Malaya, relied on them totally for their resupply, often in the most difficult of terrain and under tropical weather conditions which could vary with dramatic speed. Certain it is that successful counter-penetration into the deep jungle against the cultivations and CT camps could not have taken place without air supply: the dedication and resolution shown by the air crews and the RASC despatch teams was something that was taken for granted by the ground patrols, a fact that only came to mind when an anticipated air drop did not materialise at the right time or place.

Together with the increased number of helicopters, there for everyone to see, came a new spirit of aggression in the Security Forces, while on the other hand even the diehard CTs began to falter, especially when the newly-raised Malay battalions became more and more effective by the side of the British and Commonwealth units (one Australian battalion and one squadron of the New Zealand SAS), and 10,000 Gurkhas, two battalions of the King's African Rifles, and one battalion of the Fiji Infantry Regiment, all supported by some 60,000 full-time police and nearly 200,000 Home Guards.

From 1953 the newly re-raised SAS began operating for long periods in the jungle during a series of ambitious operations. After an unhappy start between 1951 and 1953, the SAS learnt to make profitable contacts with the aboriginal tribes in the interior and began to win over those nomadic tribesmen to the side of the Government. It was all part of the overall battle for hearts and minds. During 1955 and 1956 the SAS in Malaya had five squadrons totalling 560 men, at a time when the Security Forces were engaged in the pursuit of the estimated 2,000 CT thought still to be at large in a number of increasingly remote bases — which now resembled sanctuaries rather than 'launch-pads' for offensive operations. It was during these two years that 22 SAS came into its own. Always keen to experiment, its troops even tried parachuting into the jungle but although their efforts got extensive Press coverage, experience soon demonstrated that there would be at least one serious injury on each drop, an unacceptable risk over a peroid of time, so that the technique was abandoned before the end of the Malayan campaign. Like all 'special forces', 22 SAS was often viewed with suspicion by the orthodox units working alonside it. Its heavily laden patrols of up to 14 people, sometimes operating in the jungle for periods up to three months in duration, may not have achieved a dramatic number of 'kills' — like, for example, the Gurkhas — but indirectly they were to exert an influence on the CTs even if it was only to ensure that the guerillas moved elsewhere, thus disrupting settled supply lines and communications.

While the SAS looks back on the Malayan Emergency as its rebirth, a few years later in Borneo it was to play a much more dramatic and fulfilling role, and thus assured itself of a permanent place in the modern British Army.

5 *From Templer to the Tunku — and Peace*

The shooting war was now diminishing and it was for such a reason that Gen Templer decided that the country no longer needed a military dictator, however impartial and benevolent he might be: he felt that the future leaders of Malaya had to be allowed the chance to spread their wings before the first democratic elections ever to be held in the country took place in mid-1955. It was a difficult but correct decision taken by a great leader whose political acumen was sounder than that of many professional politicians. The military side of the Emergency now became the responsibility of Lt-Gen Sir Geoffrey Bourne, while Sir Donald MacGillivary was appointed High Commissioner, with overriding authority in matters of finance and high policy. For now it was to be political advancement and not bullets that was to solve the problems. Malay and Chinese leaders were asked to sit on the War Executive Committee at all levels, they were made to feel part of the war and to realise that they were being trusted with its prosecution and being asked to help. With the first national elections less than a year ahead this was one of the most significant political moves of 1954.

In the elections held in 1955 85% of the electorate went to the polls and the Triple Alliance won 51 out of 52 seats — a triumph for the Tunku's skill and political insight because he had drawn the three main races together in an encouraging display of inter-racial harmony. The Tunku then promised a swift end to the war and on 9 September 1955 he offered a most generous amnesty to his stubborn opponent, Chin Peng, and his followers. Twelve million amnesty passes were showered on various parts of the jungle and the leaflets guaranteed the holder would be looked after carefully and treated fairly if he decided to surrender. The amnesty did not produce any dramatic results but it did force Chin Peng into putting out preliminary peace feelers which eventually led to his meeting with the Tunku at Baling, near the border with Thailand, at the end of the year.

It was not easy for the Security Forces to understand the amnesty because many CTs took advantage of the quiet period to restock their larders, and to resume a more aggressive way of life. The Security Forces were ordered to challenge their CT enemy first before opening fire so that not surprisingly all were delighted when the amnesty ended. A British journalist wrote: 'The tiger will emerge from his lair in the Malayan jungle. The tiger is Chin Peng . . . ' But the tiger who came from his safe sanctuary in Thailand was revealed to be a podgy man who did not look as if he had shared and suffered the privations borne by the rest of the MRLA in Malaya. The talks were fruitless and the generous terms offered by the Malayan Chief Minister did not include official recognition which would have allowed the Communists to become a legal political party in an independent Malaya. Such recognition would have meant victory for Chin Peng even though, in a military sense, his army was on the verge of a complete defeat. Malaya and Communism could not coexist and sadly the calm and polite Chin Peng returned to his home in the Thai jungle. The Emergency was to go on — as it did until 1960 although there was little real action after 1958.

Another of Templer's plans which was put into effect widely after he had handed over was the 'White area' scheme. In areas completely free from CT incidents and where the people had shown themselves helpful to the Government and police, all irksome restrictions such as rationing, curfews, police checks were to be removed — and the region called a White area. Malacca was the first to be selected for the bold experiment. The people of Malacca left the dark days of the Emergency and, for the first time since 1948, were able to live openly without fear as normal, law-abiding citizens. It was a gamble for it was one thing to grant liberty to an area but it was far more difficult to be absolutely certain that the people thereafter would not return to a measure of co-operation with the Communist Terrorists. However, the High Commissioner's calculated risk paid off and the people of Malacca demonstrated their joy and the news spread across the land until, in time, other areas were declared White, but only

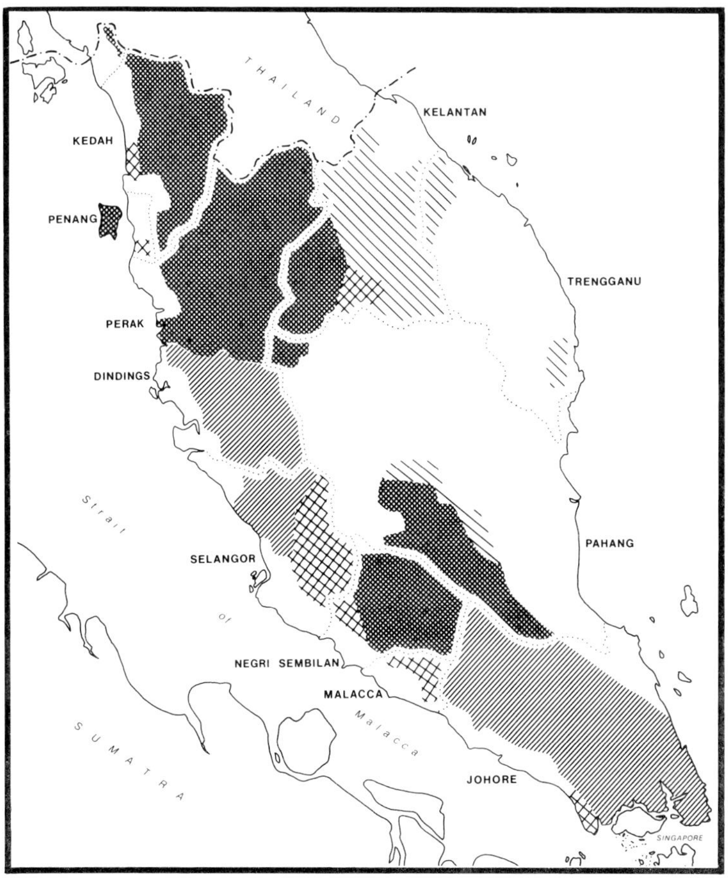

Above:
The Malayan Prime Minister, Tunku Abdul Rahman, meets British officers after he had taken overall responsibility for operations. *IWM*

Left:
'White' areas in Malaya, 1955-59.

Made 'White'

Before Dec 1955

Dec 1955-Dec 1956

Dec 1956-Dec 1957

Dec 1957-Dec 1958

'Black' areas Jan 1959

after they had earned the title.

By the time the Tunku and his Party had won the 1955 election, more than half of Malaya had been declared White; this enabled troops to be concentrated against the remaining pockets of hard core Communists who still defied the Security Forces. For example, the majority of the CTs in Johore remained recalcitrant so that Special Branch continued to produce information about their movements, hopes and fears. For the troops especially in Johore, the last year or two of the Emergency meant that numerous intensive operations were carried out, the majority of which were to prove fruitless. For the soldiers and policemen on the ground a frustrating time, but away from the war in the jungle, the political future of Malaya looked promising.

Plans for the final handover of power from the British Government to a fully independent nation of Malaya were formulated in late 1956 and finalised in early 1957. 31 August 1957 was the date chosen for the formal ceremonies and, as 'Merdeka Day' (Independence Day) crept closer, so British personnel gradually withdrew from key posts in the Administration. The Tunku was to say on 'Merdeka Day': 'Malaya has been blessed with a good Administration forged and tempered to perfection by successive British Administrators'. The British were leaving after 83 years of rule but the task of the Security Forces, Servicemen and police, hailing from Great Britain, parts of the Commonwealth and Malaya, was not yet completed. There were still nearly 2,000 armed CTs left, 500 of whom were at large in the state of Jahore.

Chin Peng's army had been fighting to gain independence (Communist style) only to see an independent country emerge expressing friendship with its old British colonial masters, and with a new Government still determined to eliminate armed terrorists from its midst. After 31 August 1957 the CTs were indeed outlaws in their own land, and always aware that more and more of the country was being declared White by the Government. After Merdeka Day the CTs fought without hope under a few fanatical leaders who continued to disturb one or two areas in Johore and elsewhere. The British Director of Operations, Gen Sir James Cassels, was to remain for a short time (until January 1959) but the overall direction of the Emergency now became the responsibility of the Chief Minister, Tunku Abdul Rahman and his colleagues.

The tempo of operations mounted to seek out and destroy the last pockets of resistance did not slacken during the latter half of 1957 and throughout 1958. It was a period of hard work, one that brought no spectacular successes; the few Communist Terrorists sought were men experienced in the art of survival with little desire to act aggressively because no longer were there the men, arms or ammunition for ambitious exploits. In reality, the Emergency had been won before Merdeka Day but the Tunku and his Government had wisely decided not to end the war formally until the whole of Malaya could be declared White or unless Chin Peng decided to order his armed followers to give up the unequal struggle. Such a belated admission of defeat which allowed the last of his jungle fighters to hand over their arms and surrender was not made public until early 1960. Thus towards the end of the third year as an independent nation, under the astute leadership of the Tunku, the whole of the land had been liberated from Communist intimidation.

Even in the few 'Black' areas like Southern Johore, CTs could no longer operate in groups of more than five to 10 men, and every tiny CT unit was on its own. Many had not heard from their leader, Chin Peng, for months — and were undoubtedly envious of his comfortable existence in Thailand.

The reward scheme was used to maximum effect during these last few months of the Emergency, with leading surrendered bandits being offered rewards calculated on a sliding scale basis which could escalate to a figure beyond their wildest dreams, providing they could persuade sufficient followers to surrender. As a result, even in Johore dozens of CTs were relieved and delighted to leave the jungle after 10 years; area by area the jungle was swept clean and the surrendered CTs taken into hiding. In Johore came the biggest mass surrender of the war, most of it being made possible by stringent secrecy and security which the Tunku imposed even though he was being openly criticised in the Press for an apparent lack of action.

By the end of 1958 there were only 250 CTs actively operating in the country so that Gen Cassels sacked himself by recommending that his post was now redundant, and he left shortly after the turn of the year. Even Chin Peng had to concede military defeat and he issued a directive which stated that 'any member of the MCP can apply for permission to leave the jungle if he is too old, sick, and anxious to get married or has a family outside that needs him'. He went on to advise his erstwhile followers to settle down in a populated area. All Emergency restrictions were lifted except in the immediate area of the Thai border where the remnants of the MRLA lived in the remoter regions of the jungle.

On 31 July 1960 the official ending of the Emergency occurred and a well-organised victory parade was held in Kuala Lumpur. Hundreds of thousands of Malayans of all races streamed into the capital city and in a great carnival atmosphere they watched a parade which took three hours to pass the main stand, with contingents from every branch of the service, with men in armoured cars and men in jet planes, together with troops from the various countries of the Commonwealth which had done so much to defeat Communism in Malaya. Appropriately enough the man who had done more than any other to galvanise the country into action, Gen Sir Gerald Templer, was there to witness the scene. By his side was the Secretary for Defence, Bob Thompson, who remained until 1961 before he went to head the British Advisory Commission to Vietnam, to be known as one of the world's greatest experts on counter-insurgency.

Following their defeat, hard-core Communist Terrorists reduced to an estimated 500 lived in prepared bases just across the border in Southern Thailand. Though the MRLA remained relatively inactive, it kept the outline organisation in efficient order as a basis for future expansion. Another period of armed struggle was signalled in a defiant statement during September 1963, issued four days after the formation of the Federation of Malaysia, calling on the people to engage in 'protracted and arduous struggle' against neo-colonialism. Even today there are still Communist committees in every state responsible for the direction of local underground work. Chin Peng, now with over 40 years' underground experience and partly discredited by the failure of the Emergency, is believed to live in Peking and occasionally to visit Malaysia with an escort. When inter-racial tensions began in the late 1960s and early 1970s the security situation showed a marked deterioration especially in the northern states so that sources of disaffection still persist and the guerillas can be expected to maintain a hard core of dedicated fighters, replenished by a small but steady supply of dissatisfied young Chinese and even some Malay students, together with a following among the poor. The pattern of operations along the Malaysia-Thailand border has continued with the Security Forces from Malaya unable to totally eradicate the Communist Terrorists: rather they continue to destroy camps, repulse raids and 'clear' areas periodically. The key to the future of any insurgency into Malaya lies at its border and beyond, and if the Thai border can be kept under effective control, so should any future insurgency.

Left:
Mortars from 45 Royal Marine Commando in action during the Emergency. *RM Museum*

6 *The Royal Navy and RAF in Support*

For the most part the Malayan Emergency was fought in the jungle, around the rubber estates and near the perimeters of the New Villages by the Security Forces so that, inevitably, the Army and the police bore the brunt of the actual combat. It was a battle of small arms: weapons like flame throwers would have been useless and even the value of 5.5in mediums, 25-pounder guns and heavy 4.2in mortars lay mostly in the psychological effect they had on the terrorists — especially when they were being harried and being put under pressure to move away from their precious supply lines.

One factor of paramount importance which eased the Security Forces' task as the campaign dragged on from year to year was that the CTs received only a handful of arms and very little ammunition from any outside source. Owing to their involvement in the Korean War during the period when the MRLA held the initiative in Malaya, Red China's Communists were unable to help Chin Peng at a crucial time. As a consequence the CTs were forced to depend on the store of assorted small arms already in their possession in 1948, plus anything they were able to snatch during successful road ambushes or operations against the Security Forces. The ever-increasing shortage of arms and ammunition meant that even when Communist hopes were at their highest, there were scores of volunteers and likely recruits for the MRLA who could not go into the jungle because they had no weapons; there was no active role for them to play as jungle fighters, and as time went by their appetite for adventure lessened.

The other reason that so few arms of any significance were brought into the country was due to the constant but unspectacular blockade exerted by the Royal Navy's coastal patrols, backed up by the patrolling of coastal waters by aircraft from the RAF's Far East Flying Boat Wing. These agencies maintained the territorial detachment of Malaya from the outer world because a series of random searches at sea served to act as a powerful deterrent to any would-be gun runners. The Royal Navy's part in ensuring that the MRLA received little of value by sea was one that was taken for granted by the Malayan people and the land forces defending them. In addition, the friendly government in Thailand, even though at times indifferent and lethargic, meant that there was no open border to the north — unlike the future campaigns in Vietnam and the Borneo Territories where the insurgents operated from 'safe' bases and were assured of supplies vital for their operations.

Only on a few occasions did Royal Navy ships abandon their silent role and steam in to give fire support to particular operations near the coast. In 1952 HMS *Amethyst* sailed 30 miles up the Perak River to bombard a suspected CT hide-out: two years later, a destroyer, HMS *Defender*, carried out a coastal bombardment on the Johore coast, following which it steamed for nine miles up the Johore River, to remind any hostile watchers of the Navy's presence. When the Chief Police Officer of Kedah was killed by the CTs HMS *Newfoundland* plastered Kedah Peak where a gang of insurgents was known to be hiding.

From the infantry patrols' point of view, 1953 was an important year because it saw the welcome arrival of 848 RNAS's S-55 helicopters in the Federation of Malaya. These helicopters gave a much needed flexibility to ground force operations at a time when a stalemate seemed likely because the bulk of the CTs had withdrawn into the remoter areas. The helicopters changed the infantry units' mode of operating in a remarkable manner when they took the place of mechanical transport which the jungle-covered terrain of Malaya inevitably confined to a handful of roads and tracks. The helicopters spelt the death knell for countless CTs lurking in their distant jungle hideouts. Moreover, some of the 'forts' established in the aborigines' territory could never have been set up without helicopters which, after flying in men, followed up with the stores necessary to construct the airstrips for future use by light fixed-wing aircraft. With the helicopters and light aircraft came representatives of the Government who, until that time, had been remote unknown

Above:
An RAF Shackleton, used for maritime patrols which prevented the CTs from obtaining arms or supplies from the sea. *MoD*

Right:
An RAF Whirlwind picks up a Gurkha patrol, their mission completed. *MoD*

figures in the lives of the shy, unspoilt dwellers of the jungle. The aircraft brought government to the people; not an end in itself in counter-insurgency but an essential ingredient in winning the people over from the insurgents' cause.

Unlike the Royal Navy, the RAF was very much in the public eye from the start of the Emergency. While the RAF's role in the campaign became all-important, it must be remembered that this was not its only commitment in the Far East. The primary function of the offensive support, fighters and bombers, remained the air defence of all British territories in South-East Asia, while the transport support, had to maintain scheduled air services throughout the area of Far East Command. The Emergency Directive No 2 Paragraph 23 clearly defined the role of the air forces during the Malayan Emergency: 'The RAF is also operating in support of the Civil Power. The primary task of the RAF is to operate in conjunction with and in support of the ground forces'. At a later stage in the campaign when the CTs had withdrawn to the deep jungles of Central Malaya, the RAF was used in a more independent role and on certain occasions the Officers Commanding RAF Tengah and Butterworth were given the responsibility of planning and conducting air-strike operations in clearly defined areas for a limited period of time.

As soon as the insurrection broke out in June 1948, an RAF Task Force was located at Kuala Lumpur and this was to be the prelude to increasing air offensive support to the ground forces thereafter.

It was not long before it was realised that immediate close support was not a practicable proposition in terrain dominated by featureless jungle. Targets rarely presented themselves, and when they did it was for a few fleeting minutes, impossible to deal with because the response time did not allow an accurate strike. The very nature of the counter-insurgency operations did not allow accurate target information so that it was rare indeed that air striking power was harnessed and used to the best advantage. Demands for immediate air support by Security Forces in actual contact with the enemy were infrequent because clearance first had to be obtained from the police for a particular target area to be attacked — in order to avoid civilian casualties — and when such clearance was obtained the difficulties of pinpoint navigation and target identification in the dense country nullified such efforts. Gradually the offensive air support had to be modified until the majority of strikes were used to drive terrorists into ambushes, containing them while ground forces swept an area, or harassing them until they abandoned well organised supply lines which inevitably led to a lowering of their morale.

As a consequence then, techniques were developed for harassing attacks and area bombardments and these were improved throughout the campaign until they were as effective as possible, bearing in mind the prevailing conditions. In retrospect, no one can deny that it was an expensive way to use air power: for example, the eight Lincolns of No 1 (RAAF) Squadron dropped some 17,500 tons of bombs between 1950 and 1958, over half the total tonnage of bombs dropped during the entire campaign, only to be credited in official records with killing 16 terrorists and destroying 20 to 30 of their camps. Expenditure on armaments alone exceeded £1½million a year at the height of the Emergency. Nevertheless, the long term effects of offensive air support cannot be assessed merely by looking at the confirmed number of CTs killed. Apart from the almost impossible task of obtaining post-strike information that was accurate, the indirect effects that offensive air support had on the terrorists were by no means inconsiderable. Special Branch interrogation of captured or surrendered terrorists proved that many of their camps had been abandoned followed by the desire to give up the struggle because of air strikes and the fear and panic they bred in the minds of the average Terrorist. Moreover, several of the major successes obtained by ground forces, operating close to targets hit from the air, were a direct result of the joint action by ground and air. An irony of the campaign was that when the CTs operated in large groups of 200-300 at the beginning of the Emergency, for various reasons such as lack of accurate information and efficient communications, air strikes were rarely called for by the ground forces. Later when the terrorists had split into smaller and more mobile groups, the ground forces asked for air strikes but by that time the few small targets were much more fleeting, almost impossible to locate in the thick terrain.

The two most effective aircraft in the air offensive role were the Lincolns and Hornets, because both had relatively long endurance and high firepower. The Lincolns took the brunt of the medium bomber tasks while the Hornets, being more manoeuvrable and able to operate in conditions of weather and terrain which often rendered strikes by medium bombers abortive, were largely used in a strafing and precision bombing role. Unfortunately, the Hornet was difficult to maintain after 1953 as it was obsolete, and it was soon found that jet aircraft, whether fighters or light bombers, were too sophisticated for this type of campaign, having neither the range, endurance or ability to operate at low level — unlike their older and slower piston-engined sisters. In summary, it could be said that offensive air support kept pressure on the terrorists especially after they had retreated to their deep jungle bases. For the pilots

Above:
Lincoln bombers from No 27 Squadron at RAF Tengah. *MoD*

Right:
Squadron armourers prepare a plane prior to a bombing sortie against suspected CT concentrations. *MoD*

Above left:
Beverley supply drop, Pa Main. *MoD*

Left:
The ground crew services a supply Dakota at RAF Changi. *MoD*

Below:
A Bristol Freighter of the RNZAF at Kuala Lumpur. The Freighter was used for a multitude of purposes during the Emergency. *IWM*

Above:
RAF Valetta, an aircraft which played a big part in dropping supplies to jungle patrols and static jungle forts. *IWM*

Right:
A patrol from 3 Commando Brigade awaits an air drop bringing its food and other necessities required.
RM Museum

Below right:
A landing site cut in dense jungle for a helicopter. *IWM*

and their crews it was a frustrating campaign but in the long term the special care that was taken to keep all strikes well away from known areas of civilian population was instrumental in bringing about the final victory. Nevertheless, in a terrain such as Malaya where there were so many tracts of impassable jungle, air strikes and tactical air movement could never have been decisive on their own.

The main role of the air forces during the Emergency was undoubtedly the air transport which was necessary because of the lack of communications and the country over which the ground forces were attempting to operate. The RAF transport squadrons were worked to the bone, and because they were operating at such high pressure they spent a maximum of six months on flying duty before being rotated. The tactical air supply of food, medicine, clothing, ammunition and equipment was the most important function, one which enabled the ground forces to carry out deep penetration of the jungle and remain on patrol for extended periods: it proved to be indispensable to the final victory. Three RAF transport squadrons took turns in bearing the brunt of the supply dropping commitment and during the Emergency the total amount of supplies dropped exceeded 25,000 short tons — a task which required not more than eight medium transport aircraft daily and usually averaged four. Apart from the variable climatic conditions and the difficult terrain, the air crews and their despatchers had to contend with small DZs, often less than 200ft in diameter and invariably surrounded by trees of 150ft or more, so that dropping was never easy and at times both hazardous and wearing.

The RAF squadrons were assisted at intervals by elements from the RAAF and RNZAF squadrons stationed at Butterworth, near Penang. It was soon found that of the medium range transport aircraft that were employed during the campaign, the Dakota and Valetta were ideally suited for operations in that environment. While the Valetta was the most suitable for the actual air-dropping operations, the serviceability rate of the Dakotas was much more favourable than that of the Valetta. Later other aircraft were to be used with good effect, such as the Bristol Freighters which also had a high serviceability rate and, contrary to expectation, the Hastings aircraft proved successful in a tactical air-supply role in Malaya. Apart from dropping supplies to countless patrols in the jungle, all these aircraft helped to resupply the static 'forts' as well as air lifting troops from one part of the country to another. 1955 was the peak year for air activity when the statistics showed that the Valetta squadrons alone dropped 4,000 tons of supplies, air-lifted 30,000 troops and 250 tons of equipment within the Federation of Malaya — all these tasks being completed in some 2,100 sorties.

The troop-lifting role of the Royal Naval S-55 helicopters has already been mentioned. Prior to their arrival in 1953, RAF S-51 Dragonflies were the first helicopters to be introduced into Malaya in May 1950, and such was the demand for the services of these helicopters that their complement was brought up to five aircraft by 1952. However, the wastage rate of the Dragonfly helicopters became so acute that they were eventually replaced by the Sycamore HAR: late 1954 saw welcome reinforcements in the shape of nine RAF and five Royal Navy Whirlwinds. At first the Whirlwinds did not prove satisfactory but modifications were carried out which improved their capacity. Inevitably, under such conditions and bearing in mind the variety of tasks the helicopters were required to perform, the numbers fluctuated from year to year with the value of this type of support being reflected in the dramatic increase in calls upon the available helicopter force. Throughout the campaign demands for helicopters were always greater than the supply and, because of the special nature of the country and the type of strenuous operations carried out, the small helicopter force in the theatre was beset by recurring technical faults.

Apart from tactical troop-lifting by helicopters, the most important assignment carried out by the light helicopters during the campaign was casualty evacuation which gave an immense fillip to the morale of the ground forces operating in deep, inaccessible jungle areas. Prior to the arrival of the S-51s, patrols had to carry their casualties out to the nearest road or track which frequently meant the abandonment of the mission. The Sycamores in particular did yeoman service chiefly because their serviceability rate was much higher than that of the original Dragonflies they replaced.

Such a limited number of helicopters alone could never have coped with the maintenance and resupply of the forts and numerous static posts throughout the country, so that in order to maintain short range communications the small, hard-worked Pioneer Force of No 267 (later No 209) Squadron was introduced into the theatre in 1954. Thereafter it performed an invaluable service in ferrying troops, freight and representatives of the police and civil administration into and out of grass airstrips in remote operational areas. The STOL fixed-wing Scottish Aviation Pioneer aircraft was capable of carrying four passengers or 800lb of stores and could land into and take off from a rough strip of no more than 150yd. Its bigger sister, the Prestwick Pioneer, required no more than 200yd, and some of the awesome approaches used by the RAF pilots would have been classed as impossible by those who had no experience of Malayan conditions. In the main, it was these aircraft that kept the jungle forts supplied and brought the Government to the aborigines, thus ensuring that the MRLA could no longer coerce those primitive people into giving it food and acting as its eyes and ears.

In size the smallest of the aircraft operating in Malaya were the Auster aircraft forming the Light Liaison Flights of No 656 AOP Squadron. Their strength and capabilities were found to be inadequate for communication purposes and in any case they were needed for their primary role of tactical reconnaissance. These little planes forged a vital link with countless jungle patrols, acting as their eyes, guiding them to suspected MRLA camps, helping them to navigate through remote areas which were often inaccurately plotted — or not even mapped at all — and carrying out a multitude of other tasks in support of Army units and their commanders. Some of the major successes gained in the campaign began when one of the keen-eyed Auster pilots spotted something suspicious in the jungle and thereafter, as a result of their reports, ground patrols contacted and eliminated 'Wanted Communist Terrorists'. In maintaining an average of nearly 1,500 sorties a month for most of the Emergency, No 656 Squadron was overworked: its Austers were the unsung work-horses of the campaign.

Another most useful weapon in the anti-terrorist campaign was psychological warfare and to this end leaflets were dropped over a wide area as a part of the Government's campaign, leaflets that promised a safe conduct to the bearer and a chance of a better life if he chose to surrender. Better still, if a CT brought in one of the wanted leaders with a price on his head, he was promised a rich reward. Medium range transport aircraft dropped nearly 500,000,000 leaflets containing a variety of messages during the course of the campaign. In support of the written word, fluttering down on leaflets to various parts of the jungle, came the booming voice aircraft, three Dakotas nicknamed *Faith, Hope* and *Charity*, and three Auster aircraft, all part of the Voice Flight of No 267 Squadron. The Dakotas operated at about 2,500ft while the tiny Austers circled around their target areas at about half that height. At first there were many who scoffed at the Voice aircraft but in 1957 when the squadron flew some 824 hours — at a time when a vigorous drive to influence wavering bandits into surrendering had been launched — many of those who did surrender admitted that they had done so after hearing 'from the sky' that some of their leaders had already given themselves up to the Security Forces. Psychological warfare by air was a weapon used to the maximum and although tangible results could not be assessed accurately, the numbers of terrorists who surrendered as a result of hearing or reading one of the messages fully justified the effort entailed, especially after the tide had turned and the campaign was being won by the Government.

Photographic reconnaissance was always of particular importance because for many operations the Security Forces relied on up-to-date information, especially when they were planning detailed ambushes near the jungle edge or round the perimeter of a New Village when engaged on a food-denial operation. Throughout the campaign photographic reconnaissance was carried out by No 81 Squadron and, apart from tactical photographs, systematic 'Block Cover' of the whole country was flown from which up-to-date maps were prepared, which greatly helped to remedy the paucity and inaccuracies of the maps of Malaya previously in existence.

On its own, air power could never have won the Malayan Emergency and, indeed, it could be argued that by dint of using local porters the troops could have reached even the remoter areas in their search for an elusive enemy. However, it is equally certain that a campaign which dragged on and on for over 10 years would have petered out to become a complete stalemate if there had been no fixed-wing aircraft, no helicopters or maritime patrols. The very nature of the Malayan terrain, and especially as it was some 20 years ago, would have slowed down the counter-insurgency operations to a virtual standstill if the ground forces had been forced to operate without the benefits of unchallenged air power.

As it was the MRLA, armed with rifles and an assortment of small arms only, held out against vastly superior forces which enjoyed complete supremacy in the air and at sea, and were supported by a variety of heavy weapons. The Government's counter-insurgency measures depended on air power not only in the military sense but to effect the political and economic measures which were destined to win over the people from the Malayan Communist Party. For the Borneo Confrontation that was to follow in the future, some five or six years later, the most notable development was the liaison that was established between the air and ground forces on which the anti-terrorist campaign was fought and won. It saw the establishment of a Joint Operations and Intelligence Centre at GHQ Malaya in Kuala Lumpur. The Centre was manned by Army and RAF staff working in equal partnership, and as a control mechanism for combined operations it proved to be a significant evolution in the general direction of counter-insurgency operations. That lesson, at least, was not to be forgotten.

7 Lessons from the Malayan Emergency

The outline organisation of the Malayan Communist Party at the outset of the rebellion was well suited to its overall aim which was to take over the whole country. With committees at state and regional level down to each district controlling their local branches, the whole of the hierarchy had specific aims and tasks at each particular stage. While it is true that the armed terrorists never numbered more than about 7,000, nevertheless they were at least as formidable as the Viet Cong were in the 1960s: if the campaign had continued to be mismanaged, as it was in the early stages, there is little doubt that the British would have had a Vietnam on their hands. Having surprised the Government, the MCP retained the initiative and successfully permeated the Chinese rural population through a 'call' system with a small number of executives responsible for each sizeable village; in such a way it was able to coerce the population into donating money and making uniforms, into smuggling food and reporting on Security Force activities.

Of great significance, too, the terrain was to their advantage: the primary jungle gave plenty of cover in which to hide, while rubber plantations and secondary jungle made it relatively easy for individual CTs to move unseen in the rural areas. Without the benefit of hindsight, there is no doubt that the future for democracy in Malaya looked bleak indeed to those who lived in the country during the first two or three years of the Emergency.

As far as the Government was concerned the initial failure to take action on Special Branch and Intelligence reports gave Chin Peng a flying start; even after the killings had spread to various parts of the country, the overall danger was underestimated and little was done except to react in the best way possible to the CT incidents. Of course, the whole blame cannot be put at the Government's door: the Army, within two years of defeating the Japanese in the jungles of Burma, had concentrated its military training and thinking on nuclear and conventional tactics for a European theatre against a first-class enemy. As a consequence, when the Malayan Emergency broke out, the British Army had forgotten most of its jungle warfare techniques and expertise, learnt the hard way and at such high cost during the war. In England the War Office failed to appreciate that the only way they could train soldiers in jungle warfare was to put them in a jungle. Not surprisingly, the military tactics adopted by the Chinese guerillas were something quite new to the officers and men who served in Malaya in 1948 and 1949; it was outside their concept of the accepted pattern of warfare, involving as it did surprise attacks by the CTs against soft targets and withdrawal in the face of opposition to the sanctuary of the jungle. As a consequence the Army units learnt the hard way: for example, during the first two years several soldiers were to die while travelling in road convoys even when the vehicles and escorts obeyed all the recognised safety rules.

The police, too, were caught unawares and their Special Branch was far too small for the tremendous task that faced its members once hostilities began. In the battle for information during the first two or three years the Communists undoubtedly had the advantage. Experience soon showed the need for military and police units to devote a great deal of attention to gathering information themselves. This was a painstaking process, requiring a thorough knowledge of local activities and eventually relying on informers, handled by the Special Branch and backed up by observation. One lesson learnt, and occasionally ignored, thereafter, was the futility of mounting search and destroy operations in an endeavour to overcome a lack of Intelligence; senior commanders were to learn that those sort of operations were indeed a last resort and likely to succeed only if the guerillas abound in such numbers that the war is already a lost cause. But as aerial reconnaissance improved, the Communist Terrorists were forced to live and move in smaller groups so that for the Security Forces large scale operations were not the best way of bringing them to battle.

Once the infantry had learnt to move in the jungle and do it better and quicker than the guerillas, then they were able to wrest the initiative from them, augmented by better training and better self-discipline. More and more did the Security Forces become expert at setting ambushes but even these would not have been successful if by then the flow of information had not been quick and accurate — as it was to become.

When the guerillas moved into the more isolated stretches of jungle, imaginative use of air power by the British became all-important — to gain mobility by employing helicopters, for logistic resupply of the patrols, and for air strikes: these are all obvious uses. But it is worth noting that without aerial reconnaissance and direction-finding by the light aircraft it would have proved virtually impossible to locate and successfully attack the Chinese guerillas living and surviving in deep jungle. Not only did the light aircraft produce accurate information about terrorist camps and cultivations but they were able to guide the patrols to a position from where offensive operations could be carried out, thus saving countless hours and, just as important, enabling the patrols to reach the area without taking extra airdrops which would have warned the CTs of their presence.

So much for the military aspects of the Emergency: of more importance were the political, social and economic measures set into motion by first Sir Henry Gurney, and after his death by Gen Sir Gerald Templer. It was these measures that frustrated the Communists from recruiting replacements as their armed fighters and Min Yuen helpers either lost their lives, or their ability to operate, or their stomach for the fight. The momentous decision to re-settle over 600,000 Chinese squatters in the long term was to be a dagger thrust at the Communists' jugular vein. Slow and lengthy process though it was, in the end it was to isolate the terrorists from the poorer portion of the Chinese population which in the past had helped them, sympathised with them and had done so much to make their task easy.

Thereafter, many other measures flowed from the Briggs Plan: the setting up of the New Villages; the formation of the Home Guards, and the far-reaching decision to arm them and show to all and sundry that they were being trusted; the imaginative decision to allow districts which had co-operated with the Government to become White areas, thus demonstrating to those sitting on the fence that there was a chance of a better life if the Government was successful in the end. All these measures were to play a considerable part in the final defeat of the Communist cause in Malaya. But in recalling the imaginative measures, let us not forget that after the initial period of complacency, the Government also showed itself capable of being tough by passing Emergency Laws which gave legal backing to the powers required by the Security Forces in order to defeat the insurrection. Nevertheless, it was deemed to be essential that every action taken by Government officials, soldiers and policemen was within the law; stringent laws could be as robust as the situation required provided they were properly observed. At no time was there martial law, at no time was a rule of Government terror imposed.

Another major lesson that stemmed from the Emergency was the need to co-ordinate all Government activities — political, military, social and economic — and the most effective way of doing this was through the National, State and District Committees, all under the leadership of one 'Supremo' at the centre of affairs.

Thanks in the main to Gen Templer was the importance given to developing accurate, timely Intelligence at all levels. In addition to the normal military and Special Branch Intelligence, Templer made it known how essential it was that commanders everywhere had a detailed knowledge of their own particular areas and the people who lived there. Individual policemen and soldiers had to understand the importance of gathering every scrap of information for detailed analysis: all this required imagination, patience and skill. Moreover, correct handling of the surrendered Communist Terrorists was necessary so that they could be won over to the Government side which could then lead them into persuading their erstwhile comrades to abandon their role in the jungle.

Perhaps the most important of the lessons learnt in Malaya — but only after several false starts — was that the firepower of Government forces needs handling with skill and with care, a lesson that has often been ignored in subsequent campaigns. Guerilla forces are seldom destroyed by large concentrations of fire; gunships and body counts do not win counter-insurgency campaigns because bombs and shells showered down with impunity may destroy several villages and kill dozens of terrorists but in the long term the explosives will terrorise and alienate many more members of the civilian population.

11,000 people died during the Emergency, including 2,500 civilians, but if unrestrained firepower had been used that total would have been increased ten-fold — and the campaign lost. Chin Peng failed to win enough support from the other main communities in Malaya, the Malays and Indians, so that he was faced with a large part of the population which was indifferent to his cause and in time the people's apathy turned to open hostility.

Fortunate it was for the British and the future Malaysian Confederation that a certain officer, Walter Walker, served during the Malayan Emergency first as a commanding officer and then as a brigade commander. Between 1962 and 1965 his experience and ideas were to prove invaluable in Borneo when the challenge was to be far more dangerous because the enemy was often well led and better armed, with its insurgent groups being able to operate from a safe sanctuary. By deliberate intent this point has been left to the end: perhaps the biggest advantage that the Malayan Government had when dealing with the threat posed by the Communist Terrorists was the fact that there was no open border as there was to be in Vietnam. Thailand, although often indifferent to the Communist Terrorists lurking near the border with Malaya, was an independent country so that unlike Vietnam, there was to be no steady passage of men and materials moving south to help the MRLA in its protracted and eventually unsuccessful struggle.

While it is right to state that Malaya remains a classic example of how a counter-revolutionary campaign should be waged against Communist insurgency, it must be remembered that Chin Peng had no safe sanctuary, no open border, and by the very nature of Malaya's multi-racial society, his appeal to help met with little response from the Malays and Indians, especially after the initial wave of terror failed to win the day.

Left:
A welcome rest at the end of a patrol. The thick jungle and hot humid climate meant that a high standard of physical fitness was required by all members of a patrol. *IWM*

Below left:
A soldier of the King's African Rifles on sentry duty in the jungle. *IWM*

8 The Interlude

Following the Emergency the lessons and techniques learnt during the long campaign were not forgotten because operations, albeit on a minor scale, lingered on, mounted against the hard core of Communist Terrorists lurking near or just over the border into Thailand. In addition, down at the Jungle Warfare School (JWS) in Kota Tinggi, the British were asked by the newly-elected independent Malayan Government to continue running the School although with increasing momentum Malay officers and NCOs were slotted into the key appointments. Students came from several Commonwealth countries and their numbers were swelled when vacancies were allocated to Thailand, Vietnam, Nepal and perhaps surprisingly, Indonesia. Little did the JWS realise that the Indonesian students' skills would be used in anger against the British and their Commonwealth partners within the space of four or five years.

Fortunately for the future of the fledgling State of Malaysia, the giant base of Singapore, with its sophisticated airfields, wide-ranging military installations and long-established naval dockyards, was still functioning: the rundown heralding Britain's abandonment of her 'East of Suez' role had not yet started in earnest.

During the years 1958 to 1962 most of the 'discerning' military planners in the Far East were converted to the 'domino theory' when assessing likely Communist expansion in South-East Asia — at a time when Vietnam was succeeding Malaya as the principal battleground of Asia. Fears that Thailand might be the next victim led to study being concentrated on that country. In the event, this forward planning was to have no practical rewards because a tinderkeg was beginning to smoulder over the South China Sea, and it was not only burning in an unexpected area but it was being fanned by a people who in the immediate past had been friendly and co-operative. To the south lay Indonesia, a nation of over 100 million people who, after gaining their independence from Dutch colonialism, were experiencing President Sukarno's experiment of 'guided democracy', after he had decided that Western-style government by ballot should be buried. In practice this meant that the President selected his own band of advisers and ministers and ruled the country as if he was an eastern potentate of years gone by, while living in a splendour which he would have condemned if one of the old Dutch colonial administrators had adopted such a lifestyle in the past. Sukarno was a dictator but not an authoritarian one because he veered from one extreme to another, so that during his presidency there were to be a series of political crises: for him, the revolution never stopped.

As 1961 drew to its close, he seemed to be preoccupied with trying to oust the Dutch from their last foothold in Indonesia, West Irian. Since this was the western half of New Guinnea and the eastern was an Australian 'trust territory', it seemed that a future threat to Commonwealth interests might emerge here. However, during 1962 the dispute over West Irian was resolved when the Dutch gave in, finding that world opinion was against them and appreciating that a military victory by force of arms would have been of no avail whatever. Sukarno had every right during his National Day speech on 17 August to proclaim 1962 as being 'a year of triumph'. In public the Indonesian Communist Party (PKI) claimed much of the credit for the West Irian crusade, pointing out how groups of its volunteers had landed at various places to confront the Dutch, without recognising in public that Gen Suharto and the regular forces had played an important part in persuading the Dutch not to resort to arms. Sukarno was riding the crest of the wave and a foreign observer reported that the courtship between the President and PKI became a marriage in 1963, although it must be stressed that Sukarno never became an official member of the Communist Party — however much he was attracted by the Marxist philosophy. For the first time since becoming President, Sukarno felt that with the support of the PKI he could stand up against the powerful army leaders in Djakarta headed by Gen Nasution. Unbeknown to the flamboyant Sukarno, there was another cloud on the horizon, one that was to change his fortunes dramatically.

Towards the end of 1961 the Malayan Prime Minister, Tunku Abdul Rahman, announced that there were advanced plans to form a political Federation of Malaysia. The separate futures of Malaya, the Chinese-dominated port of Singapore, and of the three British colonial territories in Borneo — Sarawak, Brunei and North Borneo — presented so many problems that the only feasible solution apeared to be a federation of all the states. The Federation might allay the fears of the Malays about the increasing power of the Chinese settlers, while at the same time it would offer the industrious Chinese of Singapore a rich and enlarged hinterland as a market to support their trade.

One of the states, however, was against the concept of Malaysia and that was the tiny British Protectorate of Brunei under its Sultan. As far as he was concerned, the Sultan wanted Britain to continue to be responsible for his external affairs and defence so that he could enjoy in security the huge annual revenue produced from the oilfields within his state. It was hardly surprising, therefore, that the Sultan was showing little interest in promises and blandishments made in Kuala Lumpur and Whitehall.

President Sukarno saw the formation of Malaysia as the principal obstacle to his dream of 'Maphalindo'. In his eyes, Malaysia was a neo-colonial stratagem and vehemently he declared 'the Imperialists are still attempting to encircle the Indonesian Republic'. He had fierce ambitions to form his own Malay empire which was to include the mainland of Malaya, the British colonies of North Borneo, together with the British Protectorate of Brunei, and the Philipines, all under the leadership of Indonesia and given the title of Maphalindo.

As Sukarno saw it, Maphalindo would become a giant of some 150 million people with limitless natural resources and thus able to rival the USA, Soviet Union and China. In his grand design, the inclusion of Malaya and Singapore was vital. Nevertheless, even when the President attacked the concept of Malaysia in scathing terms, few in the British or Malayan governments believed that there was an imminent threat from Indonesia and no hint of trouble seemed likely as 1962 drew to its close. Then in December insurrection broke out in Brunei: the interval, the interlude, was over.

Left:
The Sultan of Brunei in 1962, Sir Omar Ali Saifuddin. He narrowly escaped being captured by the rebels at the onset of the Rising. *Author*

9 The Brunei Revolt

The state of Brunei covered only 2,226sq miles, and of its 85,000 people just over half were Malays, a quarter Chinese, with the rest being the native Dyaks of Borneo. Originally Brunei depended on agriculture, while on the slopes of the mountains, virgin or primary jungle offered an almost inexhaustible source of fine timber. Matters changed quickly after oil was discovered on the coast and the concession to the Shell Petroleum Co at the small seaside town of Seria provided the Sultan and his immediate family with an immense income. The state was ruled autocratically, albeit with paternal benevolence, by the Sultan, Sir Omar Ali Saifuddin. Under pressure from the British and Malay governments, Sir Omar agreed to the first-ever elections to a Legislative Council for which he himself would nominate more than half the members. During the run-up to the election the Partai Raayatt (Peoples' Party), with its militant wing, the North Kalimantan National Army (TNKU) exercised more and more influence with its public aim being to establish, by force if necessary, a Confederation of the Borneo states: Sarawak, North Borneo (soon to be called Sabah) and Brunei. However, the final stage would have entailed vassalage to Indonesia as part of Sukarno's dream empire. In the late autumn of 1962 a large number of the citizens of Brunei were attracted by the idea of this Confederation, many assuming that their Sultan would become the Head of State. With such a small population this might have appeared presumptuous, but the four million tons of oil produced each year in the oilfields of Seria made Brunei wealthy: in contrast, neighbouring Sabah and Sarawak had little revenue with resources still to be tapped and developed.

The Partai Raayatt duly won all 16 seats in the election only for Sir Omar to nominate 17 of his own supporters. The gauntlet had been thrown down. The TNKU in Brunei was the militant offspring of the Partai Raayatt under the political leadership of Azahari, a man of mixed Arab and Malay descent, who had long been a supporter of Indonesia. Its military commander was Yassin Affendi whose aim was to raise and organise 15 companies of semi-trained volunteers by the beginning of December, with each company consisting of about 150 men.

The recruiting, followed by the provision of olive green uniforms and rudimentary training carried out in jungle camps, continued to take place throughout October and November. Inevitably such activities could not be shrouded in complete secrecy, especially in a small country like Brunei, but the imminence of a major rebellion was not suspected by those in authority in Brunei or Singapore, although there were many local Malay leaders who were in sympathy or in actual collusion with the rebel cause. With nearly 8,000 men in his army, Yassin Affendi seemed to have grounds for confidence but a high proportion of his followers were completely untrained and there were grave difficulties in obtaining arms and ammunition — only a handful had weapons, which were mostly shotguns. Azahari was a realist; he left Brunei before the fighting began hoping to return and take over as Chief Minister when the TNKU prevailed. He has never returned to this day.

The rebels had three major objectives: firstly, they intended seizing the Sultan in order to proclaim him as the captive figurehead of the projected Borneo state; secondly, because weapons and ammunition were urgently required, it was hoped that these would be procured by capturing the main police stations during the first few hours of the rising; finally, they wanted to take control of the oilfields at Seria in order to use European hostages and the expensive equipment as bargaining counters with the British Government and the Brunei Shell Corporation. The plan selected by the TNKU leaders was well considered and if they had put it into effect before the British forces were able to arrive in strength from Singapore, then the story of Brunei and the Confrontation that followed would have been very different. However, for a variety of reasons, the TNKU had not managed to warn many of its members about the actual timings so that not all the companies joined in at the onset.

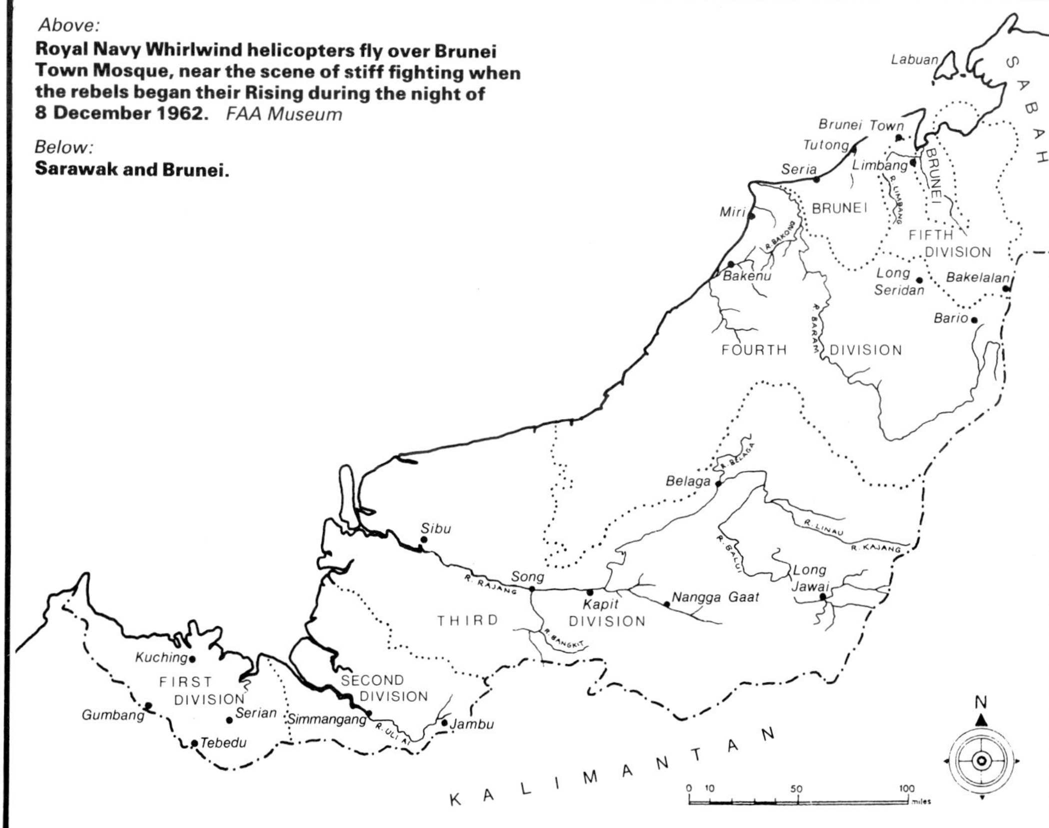

Above:
Royal Navy Whirlwind helicopters fly over Brunei Town Mosque, near the scene of stiff fighting when the rebels began their Rising during the night of 8 December 1962. *FAA Museum*

Below:
Sarawak and Brunei.

The rebellion began at 2 o'clock on the morning of 8 December 1962. The first signals that arrived from Brunei at Headquarters, Far East, Singapore, reported TNKU attacks on police stations, the Sultan's Istana (Palace), the Prime Minister's house, and power stations, with unconfirmed reports that another rebel force was approaching the capital by water. Only then was the standby force put on notice to move; the operational plan was known as Plan 'Ale', which involved moving a small force of two rifle companies with light-scale equipment, suitable for combatting street riots, accompanied by small detachments of Royal Engineers and Royal Signals. Initially, there was to be no naval involvement and no requirement for the RAF after the initial fly-in, and the only subsequent move envisaged in 'Ale' was the possible reinforcement by a third rifle company. When more news seeped back from Brunei the picture became a little clearer — and more alarming in certain respects. Thanks to advance warning locally, several of the rebel attacks within the capital of Brunei had been repulsed although the TNKU had captured the power station and cut off the electricity supply. Far more serious was the situation at Seria, where it was reported the rebels had captured one of the main police stations and thus were dominating the oilfields. Not known on the morning of the 9th was the fact that the rebels had attacked other police stations throughout Brunei as well as in the Fifth Division of Sarawak and the western edge of North Borneo. Limbang in the Fifth Division had fallen to the TNKU and the Resident — an Australian, Mr Richard Morris — and his wife were among those taken prisoner.

Back in Singapore things at last began to move with a degree of speed — it was a Saturday! Nine hours after the initial alert, two companies of the 1/2nd KEO Gurkhas moved down to the RAF airfields at Changi and Seletar. There they found the RAF was in an even lower state of readiness than they were: the Gurkhas reached the airfield by 12.30hrs but it was to be over two hours before the first aircraft, a Hastings, took off. Thereafter the remainder of 'D' Company followed in two Beverley aircraft and a Britannia. The Initial Force Commander, the second-in-command of the 1/2nd Gurkha Rifles, had received hardly any information about what might confront him when he landed at Brunei, but fortunately for all concerned Brunei airfield was still in Government hands. The Commissioner of Police for Brunei, Mr Outram, who had shown great personal bravery and leadership during the crucial hours and thus hampered the rebel plan, was able to brief the Initial Force Commander about the serious situation that faced his small number of men. It became clear that the TNKU's rebellion had gone off at half throttle: the Sultan had managed to evade capture and was under the protection of the police at his Istana; some of the main police stations were still holding out, awaiting the arrival of the Army, and while the coup against the Shell installations at Seria had resulted in the seizure of a handful of hostages, the main Panaga police station in the middle of the oilfield had managed to keep the rebels at bay.

The Initial Force Commander, Maj Lloyd Williams, decided that in order of priority his first two tasks were to secure Brunei Town, and then to recapture the Seria oilfields as soon as possible. In Brunei Town the action was swift and decisive. The Gurkhas moved into the capital with dash and vigour and fought a series of sharp actions with the rebels during which they suffered six casualties, two of them fatal. The Sultan was found unharmed and brought from the Istana to police headquarters for greater safety. Thereafter, things did not go so well as the 60-mile road to Seria twisted and turned through patches of dense jungle ideal for ambush, and had it not been a crisis, movement by road would have been carried out by daylight. Shortly after midnight a telephone message from Seria stated that the rebels were preparing to attack the Panaga police station, moving behind the European hostages as a screen. No longer could there be any delay and 'C' Company commander, at the head of two platoons in trucks, was ordered to shoot his way through to Seria. At first all went well even though they had to pass road blocks and rebel-held places, but after reaching the small town of Tutong heavy fire was directed at the convoy which was returned by the Gurkhas from their trucks. The convoy smashed its way through Tutong without the men realising that the company commander in his land rover had crashed into a monsoon drain. Taking refuge in the fish market, the company commander and his small party were surrounded by rebels but managed to hold out until after daylight when the rest of the company returned and with great thoroughness proceeded to mop up the town. This action was an indication of what was about to happen all over the state because after killing seven and wounding 20 of the rebels, over a hundred were captured without offering much resistance.

Reinforcements were now flying in from Singapore, using the island of Labuan as an advance base, and not only were the 1/2nd Gurkhas brought up to full battalion strength but the next 'spearhead battalion', the Queen's Own Highlanders, began arriving at Brunei airfield on 10 December. The immediate threat to the capital had been averted so that the most important task was to regain Seria and Limbang because the rebels were holding British hostages in both these places. After the initial setbacks, accentuated by complacency and shortcomings in Intelligence, matters were to be redeemed by two gallant and

Above:
Men from the Queen's Own Highlanders practice deplaning before their raid on Seria, 9/10 December 1962. *MoD*

Below:
Some of the European hostages the QOH rescued; all were employees from Brunei Shell Petroleum Co. *IWM*

highly imaginative operations.

After the abortive attempt by 'C' Company 1/2nd Gurkha Rifles to relieve Seria by road, it was decided that the only alternative was to make an assault from the air. A reconnaissance flight was made over the oilfields which reported that rebel flags were flying at various parts of the Shell complex and the whole six-mile stretch of coast appeared to be firmly under their control. However, it was considered that there might be a rough grass strip capable of taking light aircraft to the west of the oilfield, and also it had been noted with surprise that the runway of the small Shell airfield at Anduki, the buildings of which were obviously occupied by the TNKU, did not appear to have been damaged or obstructed in any way.

A small air armada was assembled at Brunei airfield, sufficient to lift 100 men of the Queen's Own Highlanders. On 10 December the Highlanders launched two simultaneous attacks — one west of Seria to relieve the main police station at Panaga, the other to recapture Anduki airfield to the east. Twin Pioneers were used to land the assault party on long rough grass to the west of the town: these planes survived their bumpy landings to enable the soldiers to deploy and capture, without loss, the police station which was nearly two miles away. Meanwhile at Anduki a giant Beverley landed with the soldiers standing by the doors ready to leap out when it touched down. As it did so the pilot opened the throttle and the lumbering aircraft soared away although under fire from the airfield buildings. The Highlanders fought a sharp action for the control tower following which the airfield was quickly captured. Nevertheless, is was to take another two days before the Queen's Own Highlanders finally cleared the town of Seria and rescued the European hostages, all of whom were saved.

That part of Brunei state was quickly brought under control so that the next task, the recapture of Limbang, became one of paramount importance. Unlike Seria, there was no possible air landing strip near the town, and at the beginning of the Revolt no naval craft were available for an assault from the river. Reinforcements had been flown in to Brunei from the Royal Marines of 3 Commando Brigade which had been based on Singapore Island. By nightfall on 11 December, 89 Marines from 'L' Company, 42 Commando had arrived and were embarked on two unarmoured cargo lighters which had been fitted with ramps like landing-craft. It was a calculated risk because Limbang was known to be held in strength by the TNKU: speed and boldness were essential ingredients in the surprise attack, even if the Marines were possibly under-estimating the danger involved.

Meanwhile in Limbang the Resident, his wife and six other hostages had been expecting a rescue attempt but were not over-optimistic about the outcome, knowing that at least 150 rebels were holding the town and that any attempt from the river would be spotted from afar and ambushed. Obviously speed was of the essence especially when it was learnt — after the assault was over — that the rebels had planned to hang the Resident that very afternoon.

At first light on 13 December there was a throb of marine engines out on the river as the two landing-craft approached the town. At the crucial moment they were seen but under cover of their own heavy machine gun fire, the landing party assaulted the rebel posts. The action was over quickly, the TNKU defenders were routed, leaving 15 dead and eight prisoners behind after a daring action during which the Royal Marines were to lose five killed and eight wounded. During the next day a series of similar but smaller-scale operations recaptured other lost towns and villages and the back of the rebellion had been broken.

The spirited assaults made by the Queen's Own Highlanders and 42 Commando, Royal Marines ensured that the TNKU could never prevail. The TNKU lost heart whereupon the initiative passed to the British who were able to set up a headquarters at Brunei and send in enough troops to begin clearing up the whole state. Of the original 4,000 rebels who answered the call to arms on 8 December, 40 had been killed and some 3,400 captured while the remainder fled into the jungle; among these was Yassin Affendi, the Commander. Those of the TNKU who did survive did so in the swamps of the hinterland and disintegrated into groups of men whose only hope was to lie low until the British withdrew or until active support came from Indonesia. Some of the more resolute rebels tried to make their way into Indonesian Kalimantan and attempts to intercept them were made by Army units, supported by an irregular force of tribesmen, the Kelabits, organised by a remarkable man, Mr Tom Harrison. Harrison was the curator of the Sarawak Museum at Kuching and during World War 2 he had returned to Borneo in 1944 to raise the tribes against the Japanese occupation. He had become a leading authority on the many aspects of archaeology and ecology of Borneo: now his wartime exploits with the hardy Kelabit people enabled him to summon his old friends to Britain's aid. Armed with shotguns and spears, these tribesmen played a major part in containing the rebellion, and later in cutting the escape routes of those TNKU who were trying to flee into Indonesia.

The Indonesian threat to Brunei and its neighbours was still a vague one that was gradually coming into clearer focus. Radio Djakarta had begun a series of vitriolic broadcasts which threat-

Above right:
'L' Company 42 Royal Marine Commando embarking on landing craft prior to its assault on Limbang on the morning of 12 December 1962.
RM Museum

Right:
Wounded of 'L' Company 42 Commando, after their successful assault on Limbang, being transferred to an ambulance. *RM Museum*

Below:
The dawn assault on Limbang, 12 December 1962, by 'L' Company 42 Commando, from a painting by Terence Cuneo.

ened Malaya and the Borneo states with dire consequences if they decided to go ahead and form a new state of Malaysia. Throughout the rebellion in Brunei active encouragement and unofficial support was given to the TNKU but although Sukarno threatened to send in volunteers, the Revolt collapsed too quickly for him to take any such action. When the newly appointed Director of Operations, Maj Gen Walter Walker, flew into the little state on 19 December to establish his headquarters, it is interesting to record the notes he jotted down immediately after he arrived. He wrote:

'The ingredients of success shall be five-fold. First — Jointmanship. Second — Timely and accurate information; ie a first-class intelligence machine. Third — Speed, mobility and flexibility of Security Forces, particularly Army. Fourth — Security of our bases, whatever they may be, wherever they are; whether an airfield, or patrol base, or whatever. Fifth — Domination of the jungle'.

After about one month he added a sixth principle: winning the hearts and minds of the people, and especially indigenous people. The 'jointmanship', as Gen Walker called it, started immediately after he arrived, with the Royal Navy, Royal Air Force and Army working in close concert. The Royal Navy's most valuable contribution was undoubtedly the Commando ship HMS *Albion*, which could not only operate and maintain a helicopter force but could also act as a fast ferry for men, light aircraft, vehicles and equipment from Singapore. A few frigates were available for use in ferrying troops, in carrying out shore bombardment, and providing coastal radar cover. For inshore operations the Navy could only offer minesweepers that were unable to reach half the speed of the fast gunboats the Indonesians were known to have.

The number of aircraft fluctuated during the Brunei Revolt but usually there were five medium-range transports (Beverleys and Hastings), nine short-range transports (Twin and Single Pioneers), and 18 helicopters available (RAF Belvederes, Sycamores and Fleet Air Arm Whirlwinds and Wessex).

All three Services immediately came under the Director of Operations while he himself answered directly to the Commander-in-Chief, Far East. Within three days of Gen Walker's arrival, a new joint headquarters was set up in Brunei and the Director of Operations ensured that everything was done on a tri-service basis thereafter.

The provision of timely and accurate information was undoubtedly helped by Tom Harrison's Dyak warriers, and using the flexibility given them by the naval ships and helicopters, the Army was able to react with speed and maximum mobility: as a consequence there was to be no further aggressive action by any of the TNKU. After the New Year, Gen Walker's aim was to bring the Revolt to an end as soon as possible so that the Security Forces stepped up intensive searches and ambushes of jungle and swamp. On 17 April one of Azahari's brothers was killed and another arrested, while a month later, in the middle of May, a patrol from the 2/7 Gurkha Rifles wounded and captured the TNKU Commander, Yassin Affendi. The Brunei Revolt was officially over.

Against such an ill-equipped, untrained and badly-led force, there could be no other outcome once the Revolt had failed during the first 12 hours. However, had the rebels seized and thereafter put Brunei airport out of action, they would have prevented the first flights of Gurkhas from landing, an omission which was to cost them dearly. With the Sultan in their hands they might have forced him into accepting a fait accompli so that in accordance with the existing treaty, he would not have asked for the intervention of British troops in order to restore the status quo. By itself, the Brunei Revolt cannot be cited as a model counter-insurgency operation because the opposition was so weak and the circumstances unique. Nevertheless, in the long term, the Revolt was important because it resulted in a joint organisation being already on Borneo soil before the Confrontation proper began, controlling a force which, even if small in numbers, was highly efficient with the three Services working as a team.

The Security Forces had a commander as Director of Operations who was an acknowledged expert in jungle warfare and counter-insurgency techniques, gained as a commanding officer and then as a brigade commander during the Malayan Emergency. Gen Walker and the three Services under his command were about to be tested by a far more sophisticated enemy than the Communist Terrorists in Malaya or the TNKU in Brunei.

10 The Insurgents Have the Initiative

Indonesia now posed the immediate, obvious threat and Gen Walker believed that President Sukarno would probably 'use more than words' in an attempt to prevent the formation of Malaysia during the summer of 1963. Notwithstanding that the trouble in Borneo had been put down decisively, there was increasing tension along the Indonesian border even though there were those in Headquarters Far East and Whitehall who considered that Sukarno was merely indulging in sabre-rattling propaganda.

After the failure of the Brunei Revolt, Sukarno had to seek other ways of preventing the state of Malaysia from coming into being. His first object was to separate Sarawak and North Borneo from the proposed Malaysian Federation, using tactics based on the guerilla warfare theories as expounded by his Defence Minister, Gen Abdul Nasution.

In 1953 Nasution had published a book on guerilla warfare which owed much to the theories preached by Mao, the same ones as Chin Peng had hoped to put into effect at the beginning of the Malayan campaign. Unlike Chin Peng, Sukarno and Nasution had two big advantages on their side: firstly, the guerillas could operate from safe bases inside Kalimantan and would be able to cross the border at will wherever they wanted; secondly, should Phase Three of Mao's concept come to fruition, the Indonesian Regular Army (TNI) would be well placed to play an active part in supporting the revolutionaries until, under increasingly large-scale attacks, the Malays and British would become exhausted and demoralised to the point of submission.

The Indonesian President planned to alternate military and political pressures, sometimes raising the political temperature until his adversary reacted, when he would lower it to the accompaniment of protestations about his 'peaceful intent'. In Borneo's dense forests, countless rivers and rugged mountain ranges he was preparing to pit his troops against the Security Forces, optimistic that his men would prevail.

The battleground of what became known as the Confrontation (Sukarno's 'Confrontasi') comprised Sarawak (47,000sq miles) and Sabah (29,000sq miles), both being comparatively undeveloped countries. For administrative reasons Sarawak was divided into five Divisions while Sabah was broken down into four Residencies. In every respect the Borneo territories were ideal for guerilla warfare, with a coastline stretching for over 1,500 miles and a land frontier with Kalimantan being almost 1,000 miles long. Within the country there were few roads so that the numerous rivers often constituted the only means of travel between coast and interior, a factor which has accounted for the development of settlements on the rivers from the border area back into the hinterland. Along the border, mountains rise rapidly to 3,000ft, culminating in peaks which are about 8,000ft: tough rugged country which was to test the stamina and endurance of every soldier that operated there.

Within West Sarawak there was also a potentially dangerous fifth column in the shape of the Clandestine Communist Organisation (CCO) whose members were Chinese. Special Branch reports were soon to confirm that the underground movement was far stronger and more widespread than had been thought. Special Branch was to begin more detailed investigations after 12 April 1963.

On that day a 30-strong party of Indonesian Border Terrorists (IBTs) crossed into the First Division of Sarawak and attacked the police post at Tebedu. The small detachment was taken completely by surprise and a corporal was killed with two more policemen wounded. The raiders then looted the bazaar before withdrawing back across the border. At first the identity of the attackers was not known: indeed, it was assumed that a strong cell of the CCO in Tebedu might have carried out the operation. The Indonesians left behind documents intended to give the impression that the raid had been carried out by TNKU volunteers as an offshoot of the Brunei Revolt but later evidence showed that the raid had been carried out by 'regulars' operating with the IBTs.

Above right:
An assault boat of 40 Commando RM on patrol on the Serudang River, Sabah. In many parts of the hinterland movement was only possible along the rivers. *RM Museum*

Right:
A trio of Kelabit children with aircrewmen of 848 Royal Naval Squadron. The Kelabits soon grew accustomed to having a helicopter pad near their village. *IWM*

Below:
The Army's 'sailors' of 10 Port Squadron RCT off-load vehicles at the docks of Brunei Town. *IWM*

The guerillas during the early stages of the Confrontation consisted for the most part of 'volunteers', led and trained by Sukarno's Army, with the regulars coming from specialised units such as the Marines, Paratroopers and Air Force Paratroopers. These instructors had a difficult task to mould the volunteers into efficient sub units; because they tended to be a mixed bunch from several races, including the native Borneo tribes.

The Tebedu raid, in itself a minor affair, was to have far-reaching consequences. Gen Walker reacted quickly and 3 Commando Brigade, which had recently moved back from Sarawak to Malaya, was ordered to return together with other reinforcements. A mobile striking force of one Commando troop and two troops of armoured cars was quickly formed and rushed to Tebedu only to find that the incident was over. No longer could the obvious military threats be disregarded although for three weeks the situation remained quiet, three weeks which gave the Security Forces much-needed breathing space. Based on the experiences of the Malayan campaign, State Emergency Committees had already been formed and the one in Sarawak agreed that the police, supported by the Army, should crack down on the CCO and, in particular, ensure that all firearms should be surrendered. As a result of surprise raids carried out by the Security Forces, nearly 8,000 shotguns had been collected by the end of the first week. In addition, because it was realised that domination of the border by the Security Forces must be given top priority, a curfew extending over an area of some five miles was imposed between last light and 04.00hrs along the border of the First and Second Divisions, with defensive 'forts' being established, helicopter landing pads constructed, and patrols deployed at various points, using helicopters from 845 and 846 Squadrons RN, operating from Kuching. While the Director of Operations was basing many of the police and military operations on those used in the Emergency, he was always conscious about the fundamental difference. The Emergency had been an internal insurgency: here in Borneo the threat was both internal and external and the culmination of the two could develop into a situation far more serious than anything the Government had faced during the 12-year fight against the CTs in Malaya.

It must be remembered, too, that unlike Templer in Malaya, Walker did not have unchallenged powers and lacked complete control over the police. The overall command structure was untidy and relied, to a great extent, on the personalities and goodwill of the commanders concerned.

With more and more evidence to show that several training camps for IBTs had been set up at various points along the border, Gen Walker predicted that Great Britain and Malaysia would be led to the brink of war and that if they did not stand firm, supported by the Commonwealth countries of Australia and New Zealand, Borneo would be conquered by force. On 17 May the IBTs attacked a civilian target, with the specific purpose being to establish their identity as an armed force, capable of crossing the border whenever necessary in support of an internal insurrection. This change in tactics increased the Security Forces' problems dramatically because if attacks were no longer confined to military posts, more troops would be needed. The Indonesians concentrated most of their guerilla camps along the border with First and Second Divisions for obvious reasons: the country there was less rugged and, moreover, only 15 miles lay between the border and the CCO areas of influence. Like Chin Peng, Sukarno and Nasution hoped to set up liberated areas, controlled by guerilla pockets within Sarawak itself.

On the political front, an important rebuff to Sukarno occurred when the election held during the early summer showed that the vast majority of citizens in North Borneo had supported the pro-Malaysian candidates, even though the Sultan of Brunei, once again, firmly announced that his state would not join the Federation, but preferred to remain semi-independent under British protection. Sukarno had to think again, and he had to act quickly if he was to foil the wishes expressed by the people of North Borneo. Incursions across the border were stepped up, and at the same time young Chinese members of the CCO were invited to cross into Indonesian Kalimantan to undergo military training, the purpose of which was to prepare them for a guerilla role within their own country. The Indonesian leader also sought to distract his opponents and lull them into complacency by agreeing to attend a summit meeting in August at which the Tunku and President Macapagal of the Philippines — who laid claim to North Borneo (Sabah) — would be present. The tripartite summit meeting held in Manila resolved nothing. It was another of Sukarno's propaganda gestures and forays across the border took place even while the three leaders were at the conference table.

The Tunku certainly made every effort to find a peaceful solution and agreed to a mission from the UN making a lightning tour of Sabah and Sarawak to ascertain whether the people wished to join the new state of Malaysia. Indonesian-based guerillas continued to cross the border, using every form of intimidation possible in the few weeks before the UN observers arrived and it was clear that more of the 'volunteers' were being led by regulars because leadership at a lower level had improved noticeably — although the determination required to press home any attack was still lacking. Towards the end of August an abortive attack on Gumbang in the First Division by 60 invaders seemed to indicate that the Indonesians had decided to use larger groups for their border raids.

The UN mission duly arrived and reported that most people had expressed pro-Malaysian sentiments but, to no one's surprise, Sukarno refused to accept its report. U Thant, the UN Secretary-General, supported the findings of the mission and on 16 September the state of Malaysia was officially proclaimed. A few hours later a mob of howling students attacked the British Embassy in Djakarta, a fitting prelude to Sukarno's 'Confrontasi' with Malaysia and Great Britain, a war which was to be fought along the 1,000-mile border. The time for talking had passed.

Above:
Borneo is a country of dense jungle, fast-flowing rivers and steep hills and mountains. *IWM*

11 The Command Structure

The creation of Malaysia in September 1963 brought about immediate changes in the command structure particularly as far as the Commander-in-Chief — Admiral Begg — and Gen Walker were concerned. What had been a colonial war was transformed overnight into an action waged in support of a Commonwealth ally: now the supreme military authority was no longer GHQ at Singapore but the Malaysian National Defence Council in Kuala Lumpur. This policy-forming body sat under the chairmanship of the Tunku and was linked to London through the British High Commissioner. The Council's strategic decisions were implemented by another committee on which the chief of Malaysian Armed Forces Staff and Inspector-General of Police, Sir Claude Fenner, were important figures. As was Admiral Sir Varyl Begg, the Commander-in-Chief Far East, who was Gen Walker's superior; it was he who relayed the NDC's instructions to the Director of Operations in Borneo. In Borneo itself there were State Security Executive Committees in Sarawak and Sabah with Gen Walker being a member of each, as well as being a member of the Sultan of Brunei's State Advisory Council. The machinery of command in Borneo was cumbersome especially with regard to the police. Although Walker could and did exercise operational control over those allocated to him, nevertheless the police in both states had their own command structure with their highest authority being the Inspector General, back in Kuala Lumpur. That it worked as well as it did was very much due to the excellent relationship between Admiral Begg and Gen Walker and the understanding that the latter had with Fenner, the Inspector-General of Police, based on a friendship that had started back in the dark days of the Malayan Emergency.

At the time that Malaysia was proclaimed it was estimated that the Indonesian Border Terrorists — the IBTs — numbered some 1,500 and were supported by an unknown number of Indonesian regular soldiers, augmented by local defence irregulars. They were deployed along the whole length of the frontier, their strongest concentrations being opposite the First and Second Divisions, with the tempting target of Kuching less than 25 miles from Kalimantan. During the summer and autumn of 1963, Walker had five infantry battalions as a mobile defence force to meet these threats, although their mobility was undoubtedly limited by the small number of aircraft available to lift them. During this period, he usually had about a dozen helicopters, each able to lift between 10 and 16 fully-equipped infantrymen, together with one large Beverley transport, two or three medium Valettas, and about four Twin Pioneers, with a total capacity of about 90, 30 and a dozen armed men respectively. The problems of anticipating and intercepting border raids, as well as containing internal unrest, were considerable; the outlook appeared desperate as the odds seemed to be weighed heavily in favour of the enemy and his aggressive intentions.

The difficulties of surveillance along the border of about 1,000 miles had exercised the mind of the Director of Operations from the very start. He did not have troops to spare for this important task: indeed even if he had more soldiers, it would have been the height of folly to have strung them in penny packets along the border. An early warning system was vital so that the Army units or sub-units could be moved by helicopter or boat to the danger spot. For this purpose he had been sent a squadron of the 22nd Special Air Service (SAS) and, in its support, the Gurkha Independent Parachute Company. Unlike some senior officers, Gen Walker well understood what the SAS men could do and was keen to let them use their skills as a border screen in four-man patrols, each equipped with lightweight wireless transmitters. Unfortunately the likely incursion points to be watched were far too many and the Gurkha Parachute Company was also used, spread out in small patrols through the interior up to the frontier. Such patrols were self-sufficient, often for weeks, and if they had to remain on station thereafter would be supplied by air with certain

Below:
The 'Top Brass' visits outposts by river: Earl Mountbatten (2nd right), Admiral Sir Varyl Begg, and, Sir Solley Zucherman, Chief Scientific Advisor to MoD (partly hidden). *IWM*

Right:
The Director of Operations, Maj-Gen Walter Walker, gets into the front seat. *FAA Museum*

Bottom:
An Auster aircraft and armoured car in close co-operation. *IWM*

extra items being given, all considered valuables in the interior, as gifts to win over and reward the friendship of the local tribes.

One of the problems facing the SAS screen and the Gurkha paratroopers was the remarkable inaccuracy of the maps: in most places the frontier was unmarked and in many areas it was not possible even to determine where the old colonial powers, Holland and Britain, had intended it to run. Of Kalimantan there were no detailed maps, which did not help the watchers when recording enemy movements or trying to relay accurate information back to base.

The requirement for friendly eyes and ears, watching, listening and reporting on or near every likely incursion route, was a tall order and in consequence an unusual unit was raised by Gen Walker to meet this challenge. In the face of opposition from some senior police officers, Walker obtained permission to raise a new type of auxiliary police, later to be known as the Border Scouts. Kelabits and other Borneo tribesmen joined this band of irregulars and were given a modicum of military training by the SAS and the Gurkha Parachute Company. A remarkable officer from the 7th Gurkha Rifles, John Cross, who was a linguist of the highest order, was selected to command the Border Scouts, eventually being responsible for over 1,000 men. Initially there were many problems with the hastily enrolled Border Scouts, especially when officers of the Army and police failed to remember that the role of the Scouts was to watch and report, rather than stand and fight. They were never intended to act as a para-military force and after a set-back in late 1963 — when they failed to give warning of an Indonesian force outside the village of Long Jawi — Gen Walker changed their role. Thereafter the Scouts concentrated their efforts on Intelligence work, with most of them being based on their villages, wearing civilian clothes and carrying on with their original occupations. Their task was to pass on any reports or rumours of Indonesian activity to the Security Forces. With many of them having friends and relatives who regularly crossed the undefined border into Kalimantan to trade, the information they brought back, often supported and verified by the SAS and other surveillance patrols, meant that the Scouts played a vital part in the anti-incursion strategy.

Inevitably a few incursions did get through and the three brigades, designated West, Central and East, were fully extended with their frontages at that time being 623, 267 and 81 miles respectively. West Brigade was to cover First and Second Divisions where the bulk of the IBT were based in their camps just over the border in Kalimantan.

After Malaysia had been proclaimed, the IBTs selected the Third Division of Sarawak for a major incursion even though it offered no obvious targets for the raiders. The terrain was mountainous and intersected with fast-flowing rivers which were often impassable. Apart from the few roads around its capital, Sibu, the only way to circumvent the jungle-covered hills was to travel by boat — which the raiders did. The first raid was an ineffectual one but the second captured Long Jawi after a surprise attack. During the action five of the defenders were killed while seven of the captured Border Scouts were murdered in cold blood. Retribution was to follow when the whole of the 1/2nd Gurkhas, together with all available Wessex helicopters from 845 Squadron, Fleet Air Arm pursued the enemy remorselessly by patrols, ambushes and 'cut-off' parties landed by helicopter. In desperation the invaders split up and the survivors recrossed the border, only after suffering 33 killed and with many others who fell victim to starvation and disease in the jungle.

There were lessons to be learnt from this action, the most vital of which was to lead to a change in the role of the Border Scouts so that they could fulfil their primary task as 'eyes and ears' rather than acting as para-military auxiliaries. But there were even more important repercussions for the Indonesians and especially the one that resulted from their folly in murdering their Border Scout prisoners at Long Jawi. The guerilla commander, Maj Muljono, who had attended the British Jungle Warfare School in Malaya, as well as having fought the Japanese occupation force and the Dutch colonialists in the past, decided to teach the Scouts a lesson in order to discourage others from joining the newly raised organisation. In fact, the cold-blooded murders, coupled with the looting of the village itself, had the opposite effect and from longhouse to longhouse went news of the Indonesians' brutality. Muljono himself did manage to escape into Kalimantan and it is possible that his disastrous experiences were instrumental in his superiors' decision to leave the Third Division alone thereafter. Originally his raiding party had consisted of about 200 armed Indonesians, supported by about 300 unarmed porters, all of whom had crossed the mountains to penetrate more than 50 miles down the Balui river in long boats before falling upon the unsuspecting outpost at Long Jawi.

The quick reaction by the Gurkhas and their supporting helicopters meant an upsurge in morale among the longhouses in the border areas where the majority of the tribes were intensely loyal to the British. That lesson, too, was not lost on the Indonesians and it proved, without exaggeration, that a single battalion with six helicopters was worth more to the Director of Operations than a complete brigade with none. The helicopters provided the speed, mobility and flexibility

Above:
Col John Cross, 7GR who raised and commanded the Border Scouts. *R. Adshead*

Above right:
A Border Scout, with the village of Long Jawi in the background. This was the scene of a bitter fight on 28 September 1963. *FAA Museum*

Right:
A section from the Royal Ulster Rifles on river patrol. In many parts of Sarawak; this was the quickest and quietest way to travel, but vigilance was necessary. *IWM*

Below right:
Royal Marine canoeists take a Klepper Canoe down a fast-flowing river in Sarawak. *RM Museum*

required by the Security Forces as well as eliminating the risk of being ambushed on track or river. Unlike the US forces in Vietnam, there were to be no cavalry charges over the jungle in helicopters: instead, the infantry commanders, working day by day alongside the same pilots, evolved a push-button response to every alarm and emergency, thus proving that the concept of forward deployment of helicopters with units, was vital in that sort of situation. Inevitably there were never enough helicopters in Borneo for each battalion to have been allotted their own on a semi-permanent basis: later in the Confrontation the speed achieved by this forward decentralisation was rarely equalled when a more orthodox method of tasking aircraft by centralised agencies was put into being. Nevertheless, the arguments for tasking aircraft centrally are formidable in a protracted campaign, to ensure that maximum use is obtained in the most economic manner of the aircraft available, the pilots that fly them, and the staff that service the machines.

By December 1963 it was quite clear that Sukarno intended using more regular forces in order to crush Malaysia, with the intention of gaining one or two spectacular military victories before, once again, exercising political pressure at the conference table.

Before the diplomatic moves began, inspired to some extent by the Secretary-General of the United Nations, the guerillas made one more attempt to gain a major military success, selecting the area around Tawau in the East Coast Residency of Sabah. Tawau itself was a tempting target, being one of the most prosperous areas of East Malaysia, vital to the economy of the country: moreover, more than three-fifths of the local population were Indonesian immigrants and the island of Sabatik nearby was divided between Malaya and Indonesia, thus being ideally placed as a base for the guerillas. Intelligence reports indicated that five companies of Indonesian Regular Marines, the KKO, had moved into the area, together with an unspecified number of 'volunteers' who had been specially selected to carry out acts of subversion.

Immediately after the founding of Malaysia, Malaysian units moved to join the British and Gurkhas in the Borneo campaign. As much-needed reinforcements, two battalions of the Royal Malay Regiment came across from the mainland with the 3rd Battalion going to Tawau, and the 5th to the First Division — at the opposite end of the country where they joined the Royal Marines in the defence of Kuching. Keen, eager and proud to be representing their country on active service, these Malay soldiers were young, inexperienced and had no real concept of what lay ahead of them. They had a romantic notion about war and with the rapid expansion programme that had been carried out in the Royal Malay Regiments, promotion had been rapid so that the junior commanders badly needed training and far more experience before being committed to a major operational role.

In December 1963 an Indonesian force consisting of 35 regulars and 138 volunteers did not spare the newcomers; after infiltrating to the west of Tawau into the logging area of Kalibakan, the attackers found a company headquarters and two platoons in barracks without alert sentries, and in a short time, they had killed eight and wounded 19 of the Malay battalion before making their getaway. Once again, such a victory was to be short-lived as the 1/10 Gurkha Rifles was flown in and in close co-operation with the patrol craft, operating under the grand title 'Tawau Assault Group', the Gurkhas hunted down the invaders, using their skill at patrolling and their patience in ambushes until about a month later it was over: all but six of the Indonesians had been killed, captured or had surrendered.

For both sides there were lessons to be learnt from this abortive incursion. First of all, there was overwhelming evidence that Indonesian regulars had taken part in the attack over the border and the captured KKO Marines admitted that they had been sent in to bolster up the volunteers, hoping that the civilian population of East Malaysia would rise to greet them as liberators. Equally important was the fact that a Royal Malay unit had been involved for the first time in the defence of Malaysia and the casualties it suffered led to public demonstrations of emotional expressions of hatred against the Indonesians. No longer was it just Britain's war. The fact that the Malay soldiers had suffered these casualties through inexperience, and to a degree neglect, was tactfully forgotten because the Malaysian Government had insisted that its soldiers be given positions of danger and honour and its request had been met. The senior commanders in Borneo had to pick their way carefully through Malayan feelings of hurt pride and a natural eagerness to revenge themselves: Malayan pride was very sensitive but the truth was that their soldiers were not trained and seasoned to the point where they could be used on dangerous operations. In the end tact and diplomacy were to smooth over affairs but it was not an easy time for Gen Walker or his subordinate brigadiers.

At the end of 1963, the Director of Operations, Gen Walker, wrote: 'A year which began with the end of a revolution and ended with the beginning of an undeclared war'. It was certainly drifting towards such a situation.

12 Offensive and Counter-Offensive

Following Tawau the battle of words increased with the Indonesians making attempts to shrug off direct responsibility, even insisting that the KKO Marines who had taken part were idealists who had resigned in order to join the volunteers. Sukarno's claim that this was an 'anti-imperialist crusade' changed into a war between Asians, with world opinion veering towards support for Malaysia's cause. While Sukarno was preparing a new political offensive, border incursions continued and in January 1964 a fighting patrol of the Royal Leicestershire Regiment, after following a trail which it estimated had been made by about 80 men, stormed a camp with a subaltern at the head of 10 men only. The Indonesians fled, leaving seven dead behind them as well as many weapons and much ammunition, equipment and documents. In fact, the Leicester's patrol attacked the raiders' camp some hours after reports had reached Gen Walker's headquarters that, again, Sukarno was ready to agree to a cease-fire.

U Thant, the Secretary-General of the United Nations, had appealed to both the Governments of Indonesia and Malaysia to meet for peace talks rather than continue shooting at one another. His efforts led to an official cease-fire being announced on 23 January, one that was to take effect two days later. Unfortunately, this did not stop the IBTs from making incursions across the border, nor did it influence the CCO into abandoning its training and anti-Government propaganda. Although Gen Walker suspected that it was a trick, on orders from the NDC in Kuala Lumpur he was told to prevent further infiltration from Kalimantan but to allow insurgents already inside Borneo to return peacefully; operations that had already been mounted were to attempt to capture rather than kill the Indonesians. It was one thing to issue such instructions, another for the Security Forces to carry them out; challenging any suspicious intruder before shooting meant that the situation became farcical and was open to ridicule especially when the Indonesian Government made it clear that the 'volunteer' terrorists, sponsored by them, were not bound by any rules whatever.

Ministerial delegations from Malaysia, the Philippines and Indonesia met in Bangkok during February but these sessions consisted of much bombastic posturing which served only to harden attitudes on both sides. It was at such a time that Indonesian Mustang fighters and B-25 Mitchell bombers began to 'buzz' towns in Sarawak and the situation became even more impossible especially when a group of insurgents, which had penetrated the First Division, was told by the TNI to stay put and await developments. On the Indonesian Government being asked when these invaders were to be withdrawn, its reply was that these men, and any other incursion parties, would stay, and, adding arrogance to intransigence, Sukarno demanded the right to resupply all those troops by air. Not unnaturally, Malaysia's reply was a firm 'no' and for the first time an Air Defence Identification Zone (ADIZ) was set up supported by Royal Air Force fighters: nothing more was heard about any projected Indonesian airdrops over Sarawak thereafter.

More details of the air defence of East and West Malaysia are contained in Chapter 15.

On 4 March full-scale operations were resumed when for the last time Indonesia firmly refused to withdraw its insurgents. Undoubtedly Gen Walker's undeclared war was now on and Indonesia set about proving it with a series of raids into the First and Second Divisions by strong forces of well-trained regular troops. By this time the planning and execution of such incursions was far more professional; Indonesian soldiers often fought with skill and tenacity and for the Security Forces the campaign became less like fighting the terrorists in Malaya and more like the jungle war that took place against the Japanese in Burma. Gradually it became clear to British Intelligence that overall direction of operations had been taken over by the TNI, with complete units being deployed as such rather than being split up into groups or as individuals leading half-trained gangs of volunteers. From spring 1964 Sukarno put his insurgence strategy into top gear in the knowledge that his opponents were forced to keep a wary eye

Above:
A scout car of the Queen's Royal Irish Hussars operating near the sea shore. *IWM*

Below:
A 2/7 GR patrol in Sabah. In many places a good sense of balance was vital. *IWM*

Above:
A patrol of 40 Commando RM moves along the edge of a paddy field in Sarawak. *RM Museum*

Right:
Men from the Royal Marine Commandos on a jungle patrol in Borneo. *RM Museum*

Below:
Men of the 1st Battalion Irish Guards at stand-to in a forward company base. *IWM*

on the potential fifth column in their rear, the CCO, as well as attempting to guard against possible incursions from across the long border. The sanctuary of camps just out of reach of the Security Forces was for them an insuperable problem and as long as the Indonesians retained this immunity, they could strike at will knowing that an escape route nearby was assured: the outlook for the Borneo territories, and for Malaysia as a whole, was grim indeed.

During this trying period, the Director of Operations had to rely on his thinly-spread surveillance screen giving early warning, and thereafter, by using his air transport to its maximum, deploying troops in an attempt to stop and harass the Indonesian invaders. With good reason Gen Walker was less than sanguine about the future: as long as the Indonesian incursions came singly or on occasions overlapped, then he was able to cope by switching his forces rapidly to the area threatened. But if, as seemed increasingly likely, three or more incursions occurred at the same time, then a situation would develop which would be beyond the capacity of the forces under his command. In the short term many more helicopters were required, but if the campaign was to be won, more than that was needed. Gen Walker had to be allowed to force the enemy's base camps away from the border, back into Kalimantan, or if political clearance for this proved impossible then at least his forces had to be allowed to cross over the unmarked border when in 'hot pursuit' — but his request even for this limited concession was firmly refused.

In June 1964, after military pressures had built up and the scale of fighting escalated, once more Sukarno deemed it an opportune moment to go back to the conference table in the hope that his threatened incursions would induce the Malaysians, in particular, to give in. The Presidents of Indonesia and the Philippines met the Malaysian Prime Minister in Tokyo to resume the talks that had been broken off earlier that year. While this was happening, Sukarno asked for a Thai mission to visit Sarawak in order to witness the apparent withdrawal of his forces from Sarawak back to Kalimantan. It was a carefully rehearsed operation with smart, well-equipped soldiers being filmed and photographed marching out of Sarawak; in fact, they had crossed over a little way along the border earlier that day. On 20 June the Tokyo negotiations broke down and it was back to the war.

By now the Commonwealth land forces in Borneo had received reinforcements, and as a consequence, a full divisional organisation was set up under a Land Forces Commander. The three subordinate Service commanders moved out of Brunei to the island of Labuan, leaving Gen Walker with a small staff free to concentrate on the conduct of operations. Nevertheless, it was a typical British compromise because his superiors were reluctant to give Walker an appropriate higher rank commensurate with his duties, so that both he and the Land Forces Commander, Maj Gen Peter Hunt, were of the same rank. Fortunately, they were old friends which meant that they made an untidy organisation work to the best of their ability.

By this time each of the eight Gurkha battalions was serving a series of six-month tours in the Borneo territories. The Gurkha infantrymen had been quick to learn how to dominate the jungle and thus to own their particular part of the frontier. The ambush became the key operation both for the guerillas and the Security Forces. An ambush required all the tricks of the Gurkha's trade: an eye for country, camouflage, silence, fire control, guile and, above all, self-discipline. There could be little chance of ambushing the Indonesians if a Gurkha soldier smoked, chewed gum, washed his hands in scented soap, Brylcreemed his hair or whispered or coughed at the wrong moment. In ambush, the Gurkha lay in wait for the dangerous Indonesian raider whose own sense of smell and keen eyesight was remarkable.

In the jungle operations the Gurkhas bore the brunt at this stage of the Confrontation because it was to take some time for the British battalions to acclimatise to the terrain and the hot humid climate. Moreover, after serving so long in Europe, they had forgotten how to fight, move or even live in the jungle, which meant that even after attending crash courses at the Jungle Warfare School in Malaya the majority of the British infantrymen did not reach the necessary peak of efficiency until the unit concerned came for its second tour in Borneo. Obviously, there were exceptions, and some notable ones at that — the SAS and 40 Commando, in particular — but few British units had any veterans from the Malayan Emergency, unlike their Gurkha counterparts. As Gen Walker was to write:

'The troops had to become so well trained that they were able to fight the guerillas both in the jungle and out of it, and to kill and harry them until they were utterly exhausted . . . The type of fighting, the type of country and the type of climate called for individual stamina and fortitude, stout legs, stout hearts, fertile brains, and the acceptance of battlefield conditions almost unimaginable in their demands on human endurance'.

The threat to the First Division of Sarawak, in particular, had become a very real one with Kuching being only 25 miles from the international border. As a consequence, along that stretch of the border strongly defended patrol bases were set up at approximately six-mile intervals. These varied in size and shape and eventually became not unlike Beau Geste forts, with sandbag emplacements, overhead cover, protected sleeping accommodation, as well as an ingenious and deadly array of electrically detonated explosives in various positions outside the perimeter of the base.

In time some of these platoon patrol bases were replaced by company 'forts' until the whole frontier began to assume a more war-like appearance. Companies operated from these bases and little or no attempt was made to conceal them — even if it had proved possible to do so. A hilltop, suitable for defence, would be cleared of jungle completely and then, with Royal or Gurkha Engineer assistance, underground passages, deep trenches, dugouts and firing positions would be channelled out of the ground. As time went on these defences became more sophisticated, surrounded by barbed wire, minefields and tripwires connected to mines or flares. Much use was made of the American-made Claymore mine which, from a small concave container standing on legs, threw hundreds of sharp fragments forward in a concentrated arc. An even more feared weapon was something that had been used by tribesmen in Burma and in other parts of Asia for centuries past. Hidden in and around the wire, and particularly in long grass, were 'panji' stakes: these were lengths of bamboo sharpened to a point so that a man walking on them would be impaled — following which the wound almost always turned septic. This ancient and terrible form of defence was much feared by the Indonesians, and the Security Forces had fine mesh soles fitted into jungle boots so that they themselves escaped the ghastly wounds.

Contravening the fundamental artillery concept of concentrating guns, the Director of Operations now dispersed them so that one battery might be spread along nearly 100 miles of frontier. Single 105mm howitzers were slung under helicopters and flown to the forts, and as far as was possible each gun's arc interlocked with that of another in the neighbouring company base. The Belvedere helicopters of No 61 Squadron, known as the 'Flying Longhouses', added a new dimension to the fire plan. One helicopter would lift a 105mm howitzer while a second carried the gun crew, ammunition and equipment and thus, often in a matter of minutes, the gun could be in action at another base. Not surprisingly, the Indonesians reported that there appeared to be guns in every forward base, an example of the tactical flexibility afforded by air power. In addition to the artillery, most of the forts owned their own medium machine guns and 81mm mortars so that each company commander had under his control a formidable array of defensive weaponry, as well as having the capability to reach out into the jungle and support any of his patrols that reported contacts with the enemy.

These positions were not intended for static defence alone but were used as firm bases for aggressive patrolling: platoons patrolled forward to the border as well as linking up with their friends on the flanks. In addition, patrols were sent back to a line about 2,000yd behind the base position. Thereafter, the responsibility devolved on the reserve platoons, located with their respective company headquarters. By night a regular and liberal use of fire by guns and mortars made movement along the recognised tracks a hazardous and an uncomfortable business. This deployment and mode of operating meant that any intruders would be harried even if they managed to avoid the platoon or company bases near the border.

Life was never easy for the border platoons and conditions made it essential for the men to be changed over every three weeks. Surveillance tasks near, and on occasions astride, the border exacted a mental toll and were a physical strain on the men who carried out these duties. In most cases patrols moved out before dawn in section-plus strength, a total of about 12 men, to set up temporary bases in the jungle near the border. From here two groups of four men operated separately, each leaving behind a signaller guarded by one companion armed with an LMG. Surveillance groups, normally consisting of three British or Gurkha soldiers, accompanied by a Border Scout, engaged small parties of enemy if they were seen, or if a large group of Indonesians approached, then two of the soldiers shadowed it while the other two collected the remaining members of the section as well as passing on the information to the permanent platoon or company base by wireless. It can be seen from this outline why these border patrols needed a minimum of 12 men to carry out their role of 'watch and warn'.

Operating in some of the most difficult country in the world, the heavy weight of British Army weapons and equipment became an all-important factor: many of the weapons and equipment had been designed for operating in Western Europe and were far too unwieldy to be handled with ease in thick jungle or crossing swollen rivers. Most important of all, the infantry weapons were highly unsatisfactory. The standard infantry rifle, the self-loading 7.62mm FN rifle, was an excellent weapon for NATO purposes, but with its weight of 11lb and its long barrel was too heavy and cumbersome for jungle fighting. In its place Walker sought to obtain the hard-hitting Armalite, weighing less than half as much as the NATO rifle. The Armalite's ammunition too weighed far less even though it was a deadly weapon, ideal for close-range fighting in the jungle. As the Confron-

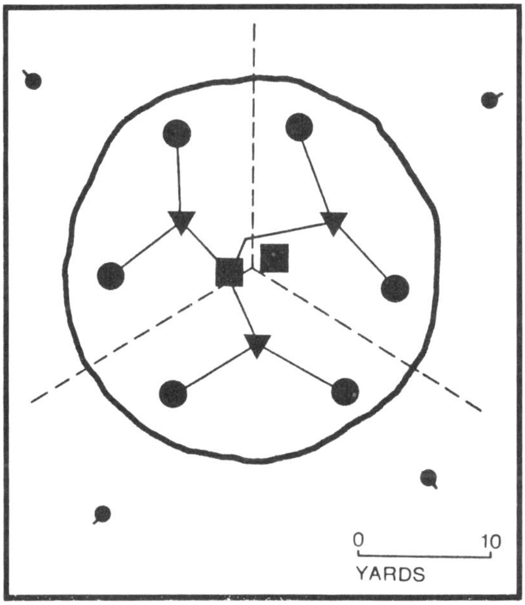

Left:
A typical jungle overnight platoon base. The ring is the track around the camp's edge, and beyond this four sentry posts are set up. Within the perimeter the round dots represent LMG groups and rifle groups (one each per section). Each section has a section commander and scout group (triangle). The squares represent the platoon HQ. Of course, the layout of such a base would vary with the terrain.

Below:
A 105mm howitzer in action at Padawan. Guns were often sighted in pairs or even singly in order to cover a wide front. *IWM*

Right:
An RAF Belvedere lifts a 4,000lb section of a bulldozer, required to construct an airstrip for light aircraft in the hinterland. *MoD*

Below:
81mm mortars were highly effective in defending company or platoon bases. This one was located at Ba Kelalan, a 1/2 GR base. *IWM*

tation drew to its close, Armalites were beginning to arrive even though the quantities received meant that selected units only received consignments. Likewise, the long-serving Bren light machinge-gun was far more suitable for Borneo than the new general purpose machine gun (GPMG) which proved to be a difficult weapon to carry through thick jungle.

With communications being vital, the wireless sets carried by the patrols were of crucial importance but again were far too heavy for the unfortunate operators who had to stagger under their load. Even the ration packs were designed for a 'general purpose' role and thus included food which was quite unsuitable in the heat and humidity of Borneo. A stream of protests emanated from Gen Walker and his headquarters so that visiting politicians and senior Service officers were briefed in detail about the unnecessary weight carried by soldiers operating in the jungle. Progress was slow and unfortunately only in late 1965 did the troops receive quantities of lightweight equipment and other items at a time when the Confrontation was nearing its end.

The Indonesians continued to hold the initiative as 1964 slowly passed, secure in the knowledge that they could attack from safe bases in Kalimantan, the majority of which were conveniently close to the border. They knew that the bases were safe from attack because there had been no official declaration of war and, not unnaturally, the British Government was anxious to avoid taking any steps that would be presented to the Third World element in the United Nations Assembly as being 'imperialist aggression'. Thus, with one arm tied behind his back, the Director of Operations had little chance of forcing the Indonesians to go on to the defensive so that if Sukarno had continued to keep up the pressure against East Malaysia alone it is highly likely that the outcome in Borneo would have been as he expected, a defeat for Malaysia and its allies. It was to be an error of judgement which would make Sukarno pay dearly.

Left:
A tracker-dog being lowered to the ground. These were used with limited success in certain parts but posed problems in the very thick jungle. *IWM*

Below:
A GPMG position manned by 40 Commando RM at Tebedu — a very effective weapon but unwieldy in the jungle. *RM Museum*

13 The Commonwealth Goes on the Offensive

In the early hours of 17 August more than 100 raiders — three-quarters of them Indonesian Marines and parachute troops and the remainder of them Chinese Communists — crossed the Straits of Malacca by boat to land on the coast of Southwest Johore. It was evident that the intruders had been told to expect a rapturous welcome from the 'oppressed' citizens of Malaya and had left their boats at Pontian Kechil anticipating little fighting. They were soon to be disillusioned when they were rounded up in a quick and remarkably efficient manner.

A fortnight later came another attack against the mainland, this time when nearly 200 parachute troops emplaned in four transport aircraft at Djakarta with their original plan being to drop near Labis, about 100 miles north of Singapore: this area had been selected because during the Emergency it had been strongly pro-Communist as well as being astride the railway line which ran to Central Malaya. The operation began badly because only three aircraft managed to take off, then one of the three, while trying to make a low level run to avoid defending radar, crashed into the sea. Ill fortune continued to dog the raiders because the two remaining aircraft flew into a severe electric storm over Labis and scattered their unfortunate parachutists around some five miles of country. After such a beginning, even the most optimistic of the paratroopers must have had little or no confidence in anything — including Fate.

Purely by chance, the battalion that had broken up the invaders around Kalabakan and Tawau in East Malaysia some nine months before, the 1/10th Gurkha Rifles, happened to be back in the mainland, resting and retraining before moving back across the water to Borneo. Of equal significance, half of 845 Squadron, Fleet Air Arm flew up from HMS *Bulwark* to enable the Gurkhas to begin the gigantic man-hunt with maximum speed. In addition, to strike fear into the hapless raiders' hearts, RAF Hunters from No 20 Squadron carried out a series of strikes, aiming at the discarded parachutes as there were no other visible targets in the jungle. After a disillusioned TNI officer, Lt Sukitno, surrendered, a million copies of his statement were dropped over Indonesian territory from Hastings and Argosy aircraft, warning his fellow countrymen that Malaysia would not greet them as 'liberators'.

As if to emphasise that this was a Commonwealth operation, the 1st Royal New Zealand Infantry Regiment also arrived to join in the operation, and within a month the raiders were virtually wiped out. The paratroop experiment was not to be repeated but other small parties were to follow, slipping into Malaya by sea while a few agents did manage to land on Singapore Island. All these posed little more than a nuisance threat and failed to achieve anything of note. It became clear, however, that another dimension had been added to the undeclared war, and in Borneo Gen Walker faced another possibility because if further raids were launched against West Malaysia, the mainland would need defenders which could well deprive him of the reinforcements he had been waiting for so long.

These landings, military pinpricks as it transpired, were to herald the most momentous decision taken in the whole of the Confrontation. Thoroughly alarmed at Sukarno's latest actions the Malaysian Government in Kuala Lumpur was now prepared to support the Director of Operation's request that cross-border operations should be approved up to a depth of 5,000yd inside Kalimantan: faced with this request from its Commonwealth ally, the British Government gave its approval, stressing that there was to be no public announcement and that the operations were to be carried out under conditions of maximum secrecy.

In fact the SAS had been crossing the border for several months, because it was and is part of its role to probe deeper into enemy territory than the conventional forces, reconnoitring and disrupting potentially dangerous enemy dispositions. This it had done in its normal clandestine manner: its four-man patrols had searched for tracks of raiding parties and watched rivers which were the main highways on both sides of the rugged and, in many places, undefined border.

Now, in addition to their watching and reporting role, the SAS patrols were given permission to begin interdiction such as ambushing tracks and rivers and setting booby traps where it was known that only Indonesian raiders would pass. On occasions, their ambushes were sophisticated affairs using the electrically-detonated Claymore mines at both ends of prepared ambush positions while in the middle the troopers raked the killing ground with automatic fire. Such activities suited the SAS well, and with typical wry humour they called such groups 'The Tiptoe Boys', because after a sudden sharp little action by the ambush parties, they vanished into an apparently empty jungle.

A few weeks later it was decided that infantry attacks could be launched in order to pre-empt any suspected or anticipated Indonesian attack. These operations were given the codename of 'Claret' and all were graded 'top secret', to be handled with the greatest of care by the minimum number of officers, on a 'need to know' basis. 'Claret' operations were to change the fortunes of war for both the Indonesians and their Commonwealth opponents and the pattern of operations from this period onwards began to reflect such a major change in British and Commonwealth policy. No longer could the Indonesians feel secure in the border bases and camps even if they were within Kalimantan territory nor would the Security Forces ever feel as frustrated as they had been earlier in the campaign.

Initially, these raids were confined to a penetration depth of 5,000yd but eventually this was increased, for a few specific raids, to as much as 20,000yd. There were a set of definite, clear and detailed orders governing 'Claret' operations which came to be known as the 'Golden Rules'. In time these were amended as the situation changed but, initially, the guidelines were as follows:

1 All raids had to be authorised by the Director of Operations himself.
2 Only tried and tested troops were to be used — in other words, no soldiers were to be sent across into Kalimantan during their first tour in Borneo. This meant that only Gurkha battalions were used initially, apart from the SAS, but this was changed after the British infantry units had gained the requisite experience in jungle fighting.
3 All raids were to be made with the definite aim of deterring and thwarting aggression by the Indonesians. No attacks were to be mounted in retribution with the sole aim of inflicting casualties on the foe.
4 Close air support could not be given except in an *extreme* emergency.
5 As already mentioned, the depth of penetration was carefully controlled, initially up to 5,000yd, eventually reaching a maximum of 20,000yd but only for one or two special operations.
6 Meticulous planning, careful rehearsals and zealous security were all mandatory ingredients of 'Claret' operations.

The control and power of veto remained with the Director of Operations: by holding the reins tightly in his hands, Gen Walter Walker and his successor, Maj Gen George Lea, were able to diminish the possibility of escalation. Minimum force was to be the principle used, rather than large scale attacks which would have invited retaliation and risked turning the border war into something quite different, costly in lives and fraught with international problems.

An American general commented that only the British could have conceived 'Claret' operations and devised the masterly Golden Rules that governed them: later he was generous enough to add that only well-disciplined troops such as the SAS and Gurkhas, under their experienced, capable leaders, could have won the successes that were obtained.

Perhaps the most remarkable aspect of these 'Claret' operations was the security and secrecy that was maintained at all levels. It is doubtful whether the Indonesians realised that they were seeing the beginnings of a new Commonwealth strategy. This was partly because the new series of actions took place so near to the border which was, in any case, badly defined, and partly because their communications and administration within Kalimantan could not cope with the flow of reports and assess them quickly and accurately — as was happening in Gen Walker's headquarters.

While the Kalimantan border bases were being harassed, initially by Gurkhas, and then by British and other Commonwealth troops, the world at large still thought that the Indonesians were on the offensive. The 'Claret' early raids achieved limited success only, but all the minor defeats of the Indonesians added up. If two or three Indonesians soldiers were killed after an ambush, the reverse might have local significance only, although in the long term if often led to a withdrawal deeper into Kalimantan territory. Significantly, Sukarno did not admit any of these setbacks, being prepared to accept them in silence — provided that the blows rained on his forces in Kalimantan were kept under strict control. The Commonwealth knew well that a full-blooded assault, made by a large force, could not have been borne in silence and would have led to a formal complaint to the United Nations about the violation of the Indonesian border by Great Britain and the Commonwealth. Conversely, it was not in the nature of Sukarno to admit reverses to his own people especially after he had promised to crush Malaysia by 1 January,

Above:
A 5.5in gun situated near the Indonesian border. These were used to give fire support to the cross-border raids. *IWM*

Below:
Supply by air played an important part throughout the campaign. Here men from the Royal Engineers disengage parachutes from the landing packs. Parachute silk was used by the local people for many garments in longhouses. *IWM*

1965: his silence was assured provided any major escalation of the conflict was avoided.

The cross-border operations exacted a great mental and physical toll on the troops concerned and more especially on their immediate commanders. Courage and skill were required to overcome the tensions and problems of operating behind the enemy lines and this was accentuated by the rigid political restrictions. The officers concerned with the planning had to ensure that once the troops crossed into Kalimantan as far as possible they were within the supporting limits of artillery, from guns located just over the friendly side of the border, guns that were often flown by helicopter to a pre-planned LZ for the duration of the 'Claret' operation. Perhaps the main concern of all officers engaged in these operations was the problem of getting their own casualties back to Sarawak or Sabah — without using helicopters. This meant they were faced with a tremendous task of man-handling wounded men through thick jungle, up mountain slopes, and across fast-flowing rivers. Obviously for the badly wounded soldier, carried on a stretcher over such hostile terrain, the chances of survival were greatly reduced. Moreover, most of the actions from now on were to be fought against Indonesian regulars of a high calibre, men who were prepared to ambush the Security Forces and were never afraid to counter-attack. The day of the volunteer was passing and he was being replaced by a tough, professional dedicated enemy. Fortunately for the British and Commonwealth Forces, the TNI lacked efficient communications, relied on primitive administrative support and was hampered by long and tenuous supply lines.

Nevertheless, the TNI build-up continued under the Commandant of the Inter-Regional Command of Kalimantan, Gen Maraten Panggabean. Panggabean was an experienced fighting soldier who had been trained first by the Japanese and thereafter while attending courses in the United States before completing his military education at the Indonesian Command and Staff College. His immediate subordinate commander was Col Supargo who commanded No 4 Combat Command. He, too, had been trained in America and had also carried out a Military Attache's appointment in Kuala Lumpur. British Intelligence at the time considered that there might be some 24,000 Chinese sympathisers giving moral support to the 2,000 CCO terrorists within Sarawak, while dotted along the border were over 22,000 TNI troops, supported by an unspecified number of volunteers.

To meet these threats, the forces available within Borneo under the Director of Operations were pathetically small. West Brigade, with a front of 620 miles, now had five battalions — one British, three Gurkha and one Malaysian, supported by 25 troop-carrying helicopters. The adjoining Central Brigade with a front of 270 miles had two Gurkha battalions and 12 helicopters. East Brigade with a front of 81 miles had one Commando and one infantry battalion forward and one Malaysian battalion defending in depth — and no troop-carrying helicopters. At this time the total number of soldiers under Gen Walker's command within the Borneo terrorities was little more than 10,000.

The need for reinforcements was urgent, and not only in infantry. For example, more Royal and Gurkha Engineer squadrons were needed for a multitude of tasks — to build airstrips, roads and bridges, and to complete projects that would help to win over the local people, such as the construction of schools, medical centres and improving the supply of water to the villages. To help the infantry units there were other Malaysian battalions available but there could be no question of using the Royal Malay Regiment for cross-border operations even though it was keen to be allowed to take the offensive. The truth was that the standard of training of the Royal Malay Regiment still had not reached the point when it could be used for such dangerous operations. In the end Gen Walker's strong protests did produce three more infantry battalions, bringing the total up to 13, but his urgent plea for helicopters only produced another 12 Whirlwinds for the whole theatre.

As a result of these reinforcements, by January 1965 the British and Commonwealth forces in Borneo totalled some 14,000 soldiers supported by 29 guns, two squadrons of armoured cars and four field squadrons of Engineers, with less than 60 troop-carrying helicopters to help the Director of Operations deploy and switch his troops over an area the size of England and Scotland together. Gen Walker was convinced that the only way he could throw the Indonesians off balance was to increase the number of preventive, cross-border operations, and the Labour Government in London showed its trust in him by allowing 'Claret' raids to increase until the depth of penetration reached first 10,000 and then 20,000yd. In addition, the Royal Marine Special Boat Sections were authorised to make small-scale amphibious raids round either flank on the coast.

The First Division had the most urgent need of 'Claret' raids in order to hold off the threat to Kuching and it was here some of the most successful incursions were carried out by the Gurkhas, in particular.

While these raids were planned and then launched, the defences along the border were being improved. Basically in most battalion areas there were three lines of defence; a border zone, a middle one and a depth zone so that blows could be struck at any intruding force, even if it managed to penetrate the forward defences or evade detection by the companies in their bases near the border. With the capital of Sarawak, Kuching, but five fighting days from the border, defence in depth was vital if the enemy was to be counter-attacked, and then pursued back into Kalimantan. In all three zones the artillery and mortars had an important part to play: in many places guns and mortars were sited singly so that some form of fire support was readily available, 'on call', to support patrols and for the close defence of the permanent bases — or as mentioned before, to be lifted by helicopter to another location for a specific operation.

The story of two 'Claret' raids is told in the next chapter. These have been selected because they show how thoroughly the planning was carried out; it must be emphasised that these raids were not necessarily the most hazardous or even the most successful but were typical of the many that were mounted during the early part of 1965. Current security regulations mean that a few more years will have to elapse before the exact number of cross-border raids that were carried out can be disclosed. As the stories of the raids on these Indonesian outposts have both been told before in unclassified accounts, no longer are they bound by any security classification.

Below:
Defence in depth, Borneo 1965.
(No distances given because these varied with local conditions and circumstances).
■18 Helicopter 'pads' for use by troops and/or 105mm howitzers/81mm mortars.
† Direct fire tasks pre-recorded ready to be fired by artillery and/or mortars which could be switched to meet threat from other directions. In addition, Claymore mines and booby traps would be set up on likely incursion routes.
FORWARD: Patrol tasks by platoon. Note they generally took responsibility for areas to their front and one of the flanks.
MIDDLE: Patrols forward to rear of forward zone, as well as watching a flank.
REAR: Defence in depth in case insurgents slipped past forward troops. Covered rear of middle zone.

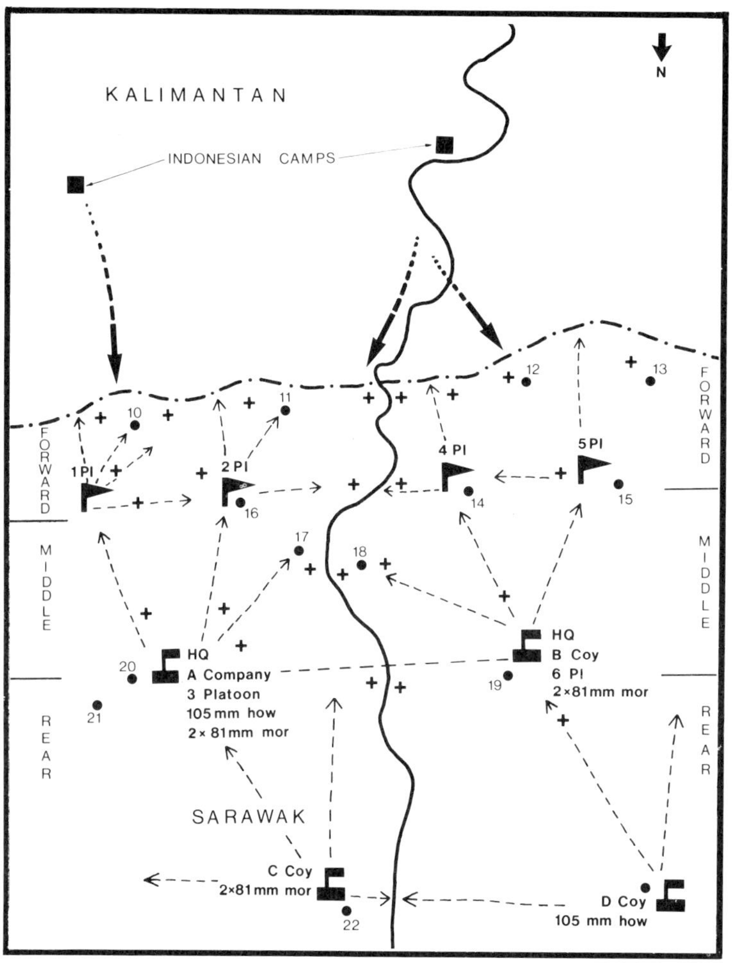

14 'Claret' Operations

From dozens of operations launched across the border, two have been selected to illustrate what was involved for the officers and men who took part in them. As stated before, there was never any public announcement or communique because these operations were carried out under conditions of maximum secrecy. Each raid had to be authorised by the Director of Operations himself and all such operations were to prevent the Indonesians from launching any offensive, and were not mounted to retaliate or solely to inflict casualties: when targets were selected, civilian lives were not to be risked. Moreover each operation had to be self-contained because no close air support was authorised except in dire emergency. There was to be no flying over the border.

In the Fifth Division of Sarawak, 'C' Company, 1/2nd Gurkha Rifles, with its base at Ba Kelalan, was guarding the approaches which ran across the border. The valley from Ba Kelalan in the north stretched over the border to a village called Long Medan which the Indonesians had converted into a stronghold. The inhabitants of the whole valley belonged to the same tribe, the Muruts. From time immemorial they had crossed and recrossed the border to carry on trading, buying and selling of clothing, sugar and other commodities. But in 1964 the Indonesians forbade any more cross-border trade, and as a consequence the local community suffered inordinate hardship which eventually led it to petition the commanding officer of the 1/2nd Gurkha Rifles to take action. Weeks passed, and in the villagers' eyes nothing appeared to happen, but in reality several reconnaissance patrols were being carried out and only when the fullest information had been obtained about Long Medan did the Director of Operations arrive at Ba Kelalan, to satisfy himself that the raid was justified and the military risks worth taking. In early January 1965 official permission for the cross-border raid was granted.

The plan was simple: one platoon was to give fire support using 3.5in rocket launchers, LMGs and M-26 grenade launchers, while the company commander led the other two platoons into the assault against the camp from a flank. In addition, both to cut off the enemy's escape and to cover the assaulting forces if they came under heavy fire from any new and previously undetected positions, two 3in mortars and two general purpose machine guns were to be pre-positioned on a nearby hill, guarded by a platoon from another rifle company. 'C' Company had to move by a night approach to cover a distance of eight miles without being detected, quite a problem for nearly 150 men when everything had to be carried, including rocket launchers and their rockets. Each of the Gurkha soldiers carried two mortar bombs in addition to his own weapon and load, while the route was selected to enable them to dump the bombs near the mortar positions before carrying on to the next phase, which was to attack the strongpoint near Long Medan. To complicate matters even more, Gen Walker's HQ had laid down that only one hour could be spent in actually carrying out the attack: this precaution was designed to stop 'C' Company from being embroiled with any other enemy parties which might move to cut off its retreat. Once again, the Golden Rules were being strictly enforced.

The night of 29 January 1965 was selected for the attack. 'C' Company marched all night and was very tired when it reached the selected jumping-off position in the early hours of the 30th. Everything went as planned until the attack was sprung by an Indonesian walking towards 11 Platoon's position. 11 Platoon did not hesitate and slammed four rockets down on to the enemy bunkers. The company commander gave the order to charge, and under close covering support his party fought through the position from bunker to bunker, using grenades and rifle fire. Opposition was lighter than expected and the camp was soon taken. However, from across the river an Indonesian 12.7mm anti-aircraft gun began firing and it was joined by a 60mm mortar and medium machine guns in support — casualties resulted, especially in 9 Platoon, and the situation began to look grim. The precaution of placing the 3in mortars and machine guns on the hill nearby saved the crisis. The

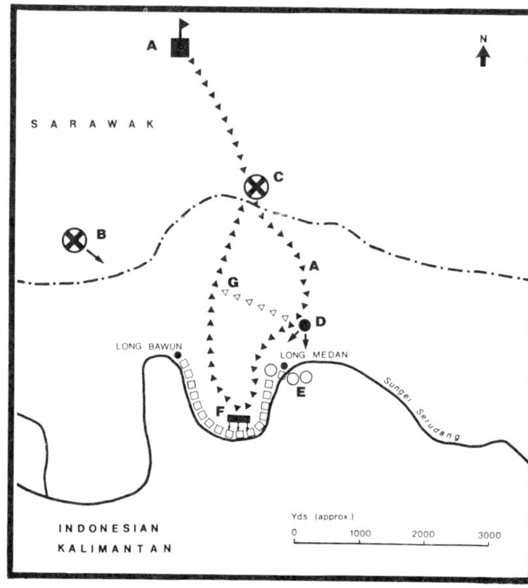

Above:
Gurkhas manning a machine gun post in a company base. Overhead cover was essential as the Indonesians used mortars on many occasions. *IWM*

Above:
A typical 'Claret' raid (diagrammatic only).
A **Company approach route from Company base in Sarawak.**
B 105mm howitzer in temporary base, to give fire support if required.
C **Tactical HQ at LZ; also forward casualty evacuation.**
D **81mm mortar and reserve platoon to give covering fire.**
E **Known Indonesian supply route and mortar position.**
F **Two platoons in ambush, plus FOO and MFC.**
G **Direct withdrawal route after ambush sprung.**

Below:
Ba Kelalan longhouses where a company of 1/2 Gurkha Rifles had a base among the local Murut inhabitants. It was from here that the 'Claret' raid was launched. *AAC Museum*

Mortar Fire Controller (MFC), a corporal who was to win the Military Medal, had to stand up and expose himself to the Indonesian machine gun fire while making quick calculations. He was able to pinpoint the hostile 60mm mortar position and, after a ranging round, his second bomb blew the mortar up and killed the crew. He then turned his attention to the Indonesian machine guns and knocked them out.

Meanwhile the 12.7mm gun remained in action, firing tracer rounds which pinned the forward section down and threatened to cause more casualties. In retaliation 12 Platoon sent a corporal and two riflemen to silence the gun, and after taking a rocket launcher across a paddyfield they stealthily approached the gun post while the rest of the platoon kept up a noisy diversionary fire attack. A few minutes later the corporal opened fire and the first rocket hit the gun pit, killing its occupants. That was to be the end of the battle.

It had taken one hour and 15 minutes — 15 minutes over the time allowed so the company commander ordered an immediate withdrawal. By late afternoon, using a more direct route, the raiding force was back across the border, carrying two of its badly wounded men with it as well as the body of a dead Gurkha rifleman. A few days later it was confirmed that 50% of the Indonesian strength in that area had been killed. Of far more importance was the fact that Long Medan was never reoccupied, and as a consequence no further raids were made across the border by the Indonesians in the Ba Kelalan area during the Confrontation. For his cool leadership throughout this well-planned operation, the young company commander was awarded the Military Cross.

A few months later, in November 1965, another company from the sister battalion of the 2nd Gurkhas was given a 'Claret' mission opposite the First Division of Sarawak. This time it was to be Support Company which carried out a full day of preparations, rehearsed weapon testing and other necessary techniques before moving off at first light on its operation. The company's mission was to ambush the main river supply route at two points near one of the Indonesians' company-sized bases. This was a much more ambitious operation than the one at Long Medan because it would take the raiding party over two days even to get close to the target area. As a consequence each man carried light rations to last for 12 days on his back, apart from his personal weapon, ammunition and other vital necessities.

Support Company moved down the almost precipitous slope leading into Kalimantan — a long line of heavily burdened men, many of them with headbands over their foreheads helping to take the weight of their 100lb packs. The going was very difficult so that short breaks had to be taken every hour. At the end of the first day they had made reasonable progress without any signs of the TNI or any civilians. Nevertheless, the company commander, being an experienced officer, ordered slit trenches to be dug for the night's stay as, on a previous operation, his company had been heavily mortared at night and the lesson had been learnt. Next day two rivers were met in succession and each time the Assault Pioneers, after lashing a tree at the top with a long rope, sawed through its base with a folding saw before, like a ship's derrick, it was dropped over the river. Once the tree was in position, a Gurkha soldier went across with two ropes, securing these to trees on the other side so that the company was able to file over, using them as hand-ropes. After the last man was over, the 'bridge' was hauled up, pulled out of sight and the white sawn wood covered with mud to hide it. It was an efficient way of crossing rivers but inevitably it took time.

A day later the company had reached an area near the River Separan. Patrols had reported the area as being thick primary jungle with a fast-flowing river which was about 25m wide. The company commander, realising he would be ambushing between two large Indonesian camps, crossed the final river with great care. The Assault Pioneer Platoon was left behind to cover the rear while the remainder of the company crossed unseen and set its ambush on a track with a telegraph wire above it which linked the two enemy camps. The company commander placed himself and the Anti-Tank Platoon in the ambush area, while the Reconnaissance Platoon and the Forward Observation Officer (FOO), from the artillery, remained on the other side of the river, in order to protect the rear and to cover the 'tree-bridge'. The FOO by using his communications could assist the troops by bringing down diversionary fire on the approaches to the ambush as soon as it was sprung; the plan included clear orders about who would open fire. Then it was just a question of waiting patiently. All were in position and ready by 09.45hrs.

Just after 11.00hrs the company commander received the signal for 'Enemy' and about five minutes later three Indonesians, wearing steel helmets and dark olive drab uniforms, walked nonchalently through the ambush zone from the south. The Gurkhas let them go. Seconds later another signal for more 'Enemy' was received and five more walked by, followed by another six and then came a continuous line. It was time to spring the ambush. GPMGs opened up on the one flank followed by the crash of Claymore mines which had been laid on the other end of the ambush zone. Simultaneously all the waiting ambushers opened fire at targets in front of them and about a minute or two later artillery shells crashed down on either side of the main ambush position. At first the shock ambush completely stunned the Indonesian soldiers but it was not long before a counter-attack swung in from the south, covered by mortar fire from a post close by. Support Company's well-planned position held firm and the Indonesian counter-attack was an abortive one. Quickly checking the enemy casualties — 11 soldiers had been killed and counted while several more were hit and fell out of sight in the jungle — the company commander decided it was time to withdraw before the Indonesians regained the initiative once more. On his instructions men from the right flank of the ambush went across the 'bridge', then the centre, then finally the five remaining men on the left flank joined up with the company commander and moved safely over the makeshift bridge. After a rapid check that everyone was present, the Assault Pioneers pulled away the lashings holding the tree which sprung out into mid-stream to float away. At the same time the FOO directed his guns on to shelling the immediate area of the abandoned ambush position.

There was no time to dawdle. The company set off and pressed on hard till dark. Next day, the fifth day after setting out, it recrossed the border and was safe in 'home' territory. Subsequently air photographs were taken of the position and these confirmed that there had been two enemy camps, one to the south and the other less than a mile to the north of the ambush position selected by Support Company: that the Gurkhas got away was almost a miracle. It had been a model operation, well planned and expertly executed, and as a result the Indonesians in that particular area took no more offensive action during the rest of the Confrontation. Once again, the company commander who had carried a heavy responsibility on his shoulders by leading his men into Indonesian territory and deciding when to strike and where — and even more difficult, when to withdraw — richly deserved the Military Cross awarded for his leadership during this operation.

By early 1966 the Confrontation in the military sense had been won by British and Commonwealth soldiers operating along and over the border. That victory had been achieved against numerically superior forces was due in no small way to the 'Claret' operations. The TNI and volunteers lost the initiative, and once they were forced to abandon their forward camps and bases then defeat was inevitable. The cross-border operations mounted under the stringent Golden Rules proved to be the turning point of a fascinating campaign, one that was waged under wraps of secrecy. In a media-conscious world, that in itself made the Borneo Confrontation unique.

Above:
Men of the 2/2 GR on their raid into Indonesia.
Author/Bullock

15 Use of Air Power to Defeat the Jungle

On 8 December 1962, the day the Brunei Revolt broke out, the Far East Air Force (FEAF) was fortunate in having more transport and heavy aircraft available than usual — by chance rather than due to any planning, because the timing and the nature of the insurrection was a complete surprise to everyone in Singapore, including GHQ FARELF. Consequently, 8 December was a difficult day for the Army as well as the Royal Air Force, but by commandeering a Britannia from Transport Command which was on the ground at RAF Changi, matters were eased somewhat, although the plane had to land at Labuan because there was no airfield in Brunei State capable of accepting such an aircraft. After 9 December full credit must be given to FEAF for speed and improvision: during the 8th and 9th, 28 transport aircraft loads were flown into Brunei while at the same time the vital staging post was built up to cope with the heavy traffic. Every available aircraft was pressed into service including a Bristol Freighter from the RNZAF and a Hercules C-130 from the RAAF. It was a hectic period during which all concerned worked hard around the clock so that by the 13th day after the Revolt had started, the airlift had taken over 3,000 passengers, 113 vehicles, assorted guns and trailers, and two Auster aircraft into Brunei. All this entailed a tremendous strain on the small and hastily constituted staging post detachment at Labuan.

The special operation against Seria, mounted by the Queen's Own Highlanders on 10 December, has already been mentioned, but it must be emphasised that the soldiers could not have carried out their most successful coup de main without the intrepid pilots of five Twin Pioneers of No 209 Squadron and the single Beverley from No 34 Squadron. All the aircraft returned safely to base although the gallant Beverley was hit twice in the rear fuselage. Clearing the Shell Oil complex in Seria had to be done by the Army without air strikes — for obvious reasons — but the ground force received considerable psychological help when four Hunters of No 20 Squadron staged a mock attack on Seria police station to frighten the TNKU, which was followed by a broadcast from a No 209 Squadron Voice Pioneer, calling on the demoralised rebels to surrender.

Once the main TNKU insurrection had been broken, RAF Beverleys played a big part in all-important 'hearts and minds' campaign, and particularly after New Year 1963 when the small state experienced some dramatic flooding and countless villages were isolated by the swirling waters. Food supplies were parachuted to towns and settlements, a humanitarian operation which indirectly influenced the local population into supporting Britain as well as inducing the fugitive rebels into surrendering. By the time the Confrontation in Borneo had begun, FEAF was in a much stronger position to ensure the inviolability of the new state of Malaysia from hostile air power: the joint headquarters, the establishment of which had initially met with some opposition from the Royal Navy and RAF, had been set up and was working well with the necessary signal communications, while the staging post at Labuan was to grow from 78 personnel to about 500 before the year was out. On the face of it, therefore, the Royal Air Force was readily placed to give maximum support to the ground forces operating along the border with Kalimantan: the main problems to be encountered and overcome were the flying conditions and terrain that existed in Borneo, rather than the threat posed by the Indonesian Air Force.

In most parts of the interior a thick mist remained until about 10am, to be followed by a clear period of good flying weather which lasted for four to five hours. Thereafter there was a gradual build-up of cloud which in the mountainous regions meant that there could be bouts of violent turbulence and severe down draughts, testing the skills of even the most experienced of pilots. As a consequence tactical air operations were usually confined to a few hours in the middle of the day, while to operate at night, especially among the mountains and hills, was impracticable even if it had proved possible to locate targets. The weather could change with dramatic speed and did so many times.

Above:
Floods in Brunei during January 1963, when the Security Forces dropped supplies to outlying villages and hamlets.
FAA Museum

Right:
What a crewman could see, flying in a Belvedere from No 66 Squadron RAF. *MoD*

To add to the meteorological problems, there was the fact that accurate mapping and survey of most parts of the country was virtually non-existent and the few small-scale maps available were of little value when tactical flying had to be carried out. This meant that pilots and navigators were compelled to adopt a form of contour navigation to a target area, being forced to rely very much on their personal knowledge of the main features such as prominent ridges, large rivers and distinctive valleys. It soon became clear that experience in the theatre of operations counted for everything and that there was no merit to rotating air crews too quickly — continuity was all-important.

The third factor that must be remembered was distance, with Labuan being some 400 miles from the FEAF airfields in Singapore, while away to the east Tawau was over 1,300 miles from the main base of all the aircraft involved. Much flying time was spent in even reaching the target area so that the island of Labuan was ideally situated, and without it the level of air support that was maintained would not have been possible.

After Malaysia had been proclaimed on 19 September 1963, the burning down of the British Embassy and the anti-British sentiments expressed by the volatile students necessitated the sudden evacuation of 400 British nationals from Djakarta to Singapore, the airlift being mounted by three Argosies and one Hastings from No 48 Squadron. Although this exodus went without any major hitch, it was to have an important consequence because thereafter there could be no more flying over Indonesian air space — which for aircraft bound for Australia meant considerable inconvenience and an unwelcome increase in flying time. On the other hand it did not prevent the Indonesian Air Force from flying over Malaysian territory, and during November 1964 there were nine reported incursions made by B-25 Mitchell bombers, escorted by P-51 Mustang fighters.

It is now time to look at the Indonesian Air Force as it was during the Confrontation period. Numerically strong, Sukarno's air force consisted of 550 aircraft but the machines were of mixed national origin and of varying vintage. There were a few Russian 'Badgers', United States B-25 Mitchells, while the fighter squadrons ranged from P-51 Mustang fighters to some old Russian MiG-17s, 19s and 21s. Likewise the transport support fleet was a hybrid one, mainly depending on C-130 Hercules and some ancient Dakotas, while the helicopters were of Russian origin, often without the necessary spares. On numbers alone, the Indonesian Air Force was one to be respected but as the Confrontation went on it became clear that the Indonesian pilots had a wholesome respect for their RAF opponents; once it was known that RAF fighters had been 'scrambled', evasion tactics were adopted on every occasion, all of which proved successful as no aircraft were shot down by either side during the whole period of hostilities. Thus by exercising its complete superiority in the air, the RAF ensured that the Commonwealth troops were given maximum, effective logistic support — in contrast to the Indonesian troops in Kalimantan who had to fight the campaign at the end of a long and tenuous shoestring, invariably relying on local boats operating on the rivers which were often dangerous after heavy rains.

The incursions by the Indonesian aircraft meant that an Air Defence Identification Zone (ADIZ) was set up immediately afterwards which not only covered the length of the border but extended to a distance of three miles off-shore as well. In order to police this ADIZ eight Hunters were detached from No 20 Squadron and stationed on Borneo soil — four at Labuan and four at Kuching. Later, in order to establish a permanent all-weather day and night vigil, two Javelins from No 64 Squadron were positioned at both airports. With the border being so near Kuching, there was no possibility of pilots seeking guidance from higher authority, should an Indonesian incursion by air take place, so that the rules of engagement allowed pilots to attack and destroy any hostile aircraft over-flying the ADIZ, without first having to obtain permission from ground control after the aircraft sighting. The aim was to deter the Indonesian Air Force from entering Borneo air space and the addition of Mark MR Javelins, carrying long range fuel tanks and Firestreak air-to-air missiles, made No 60 Squadron a formidable force — not surprisingly there was a temporary reduction of violations of air space by Indonesia for an appreciable period after these aircraft went into operational service.

After Malaysia had been proclaimed, there was a steady, albeit modest, build-up in the ground and air forces under Gen Walker's command. All this led to two ever-increasing commitments for the air transport support: firstly, the resupply by air of more patrols and static posts, and secondly, as the campaign increased in tempo, the rotation of units in the forward areas which had to be carried out with speed for reasons which are described in a later paragraph.

As far as air resupply was concerned, Labuan and Kuching were the two forward airfields to where a stream of aircraft daily flew in the supplies, equipment and personnel urgently required in the theatre: the aircraft used for this link in the supply chain were Hastings, Argosies and Beverleys, assisted by RNZAF Bristol Freighters. Thence, Pioneer aircraft from No 209 Squadron and Belvederes from No 66 Squadron had the task of taking personnel and items required in a hurry to the rough and ready airstrips that had been

Above:
A Hunter from No 20 Squadron RAF over Borneo. This squadron's presence there helped stop the Indonesian Air Force from making any serious air incursion.
Brian H. Lawrence

Below:
RAF Gloster Javelins of No 60 Squadron. Detachments on a semi-permanent basis were operating from the Borneo Territories. *MoD*

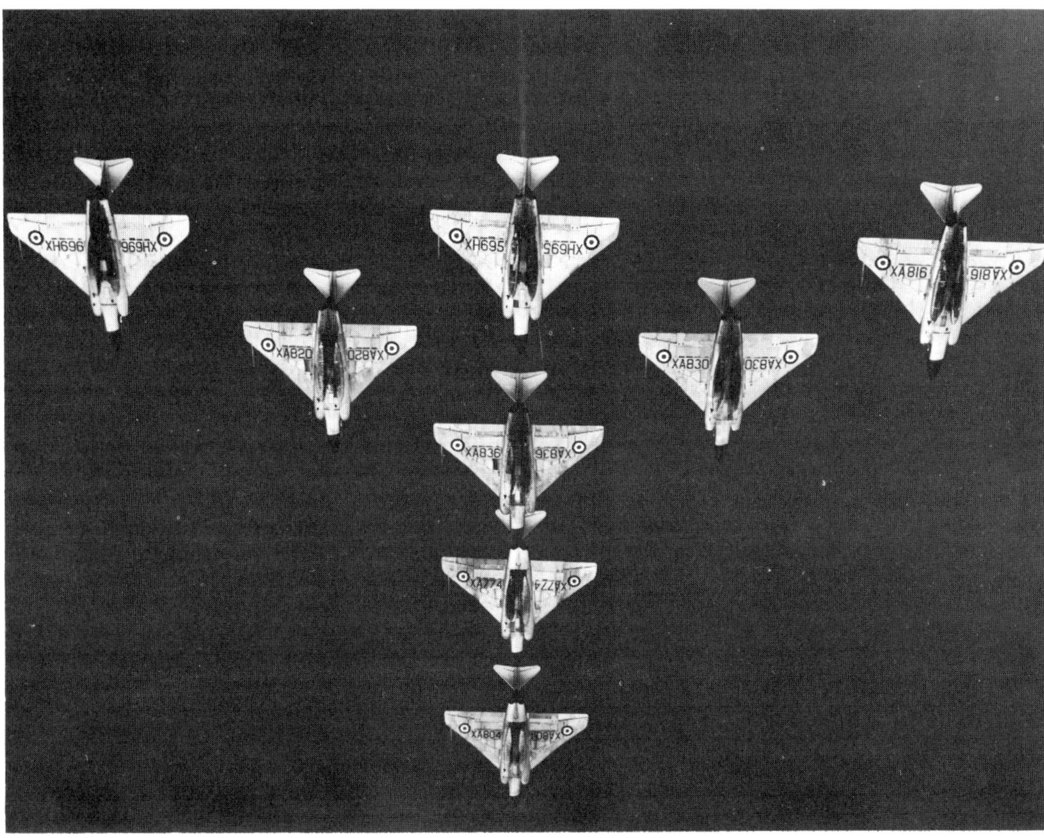

established in the forward areas, usually close to the border, which meant that they had to be defended by ground forces. In certain areas, however, supplies could not be air landed and were dropped by parachute using the medium-range aircraft operating from either Labuan or Kuching. Supplementing the aircraft used on air supply were the workhorses of the campaign, the helicopters. There were never enough of these but welcome reinforcements were received when No 225 Squadron, equipped with Whirlwind 10s and No 26 Squadron, consisting of four Belvederes, were whisked away from Exercise 'Triplex West' in the Middle East and taken by HMS *Albion* from El Adem to the Far East where they joined the already heavily committed detachments from Nos 110, 66 and 103 Squadrons. Their arrival doubled the total number of helicopters available to the Commonwealth forces in Borneo.

The helicopters, from all three Services, became an all-important weapon in the Director of Operations' strategy and were used for a multitude of military purposes from tactical to administrative and, when the situation permitted, to occasionally help the local people living in isolated longhouses. At the height of Confrontation there were usually about 50 machines serviceable and working at maximum pitch. The Belvederes from No 66 Squadron, detached to Kuching, proved invaluable on a number of occasions because they were able to increase the mobility and range of the 105mm guns and mortars, dotted around the forward positions. As explained earlier, one helicopter would pick up a 105mm gun while the second carried its equipment, ammunition and the gun crews. By so doing, every cross-border operation was promised fire support 'on call', while the moving of guns from one company position to another led the Indonesians into thinking that there were many more guns opposed to them than there actually were in the forward posts. In addition, Belvederes were able to rescue one or two smaller helicopters which had either crashed or had become unserviceable in the forward areas, to lift them back to base for repair.

Under the umbrella of complete air supremacy the British and Commonwealth troops were able to concentrate on their tactical operations in the knowledge that supplies and ammunition would arrive as near to the time and place as weather conditions allowed. The tempo of activity rose sharply until by December 1964 one million pounds of supplies were dropped in that month alone, and the total continued to rise thereafter.

A major air commitment was involved each time battalions were relieved after completing a six-month tour because there was never enough accommodation to meet the needs of the incoming and outgoing units in the Forward Defence Locality (FDL). Because units could not overlap, it meant that a most complicated movement plot had to be devised for each change-round. To add to the complexity of the planning there were no airstrips in the forward areas capable of accepting long-range aircraft so that incoming personnel had to be shuttled forward over the last stage, using the faithful Pioneers and helicopters which then returned with men from the outgoing unit. In general these unit reliefs went extremely well although inevitably there were hitches, particularly when the weather suddenly deteriorated or one or two of the aircraft became unserviceable. Each relief posed a different set of problems to the Movements staff, sometimes taxing their ability to improvise to the limit.

While all these operations continued day by day, the Canberras from No 81 Squadron, operating from RAF Tengah in Singapore and using Labuan as an advance base, were carrying out extensive photography and survey along the whole border. With indifferent and sometimes inaccurate maps, it was vital that the soldiers and airmen, of all three Services, who had to police the border were given accurate maps and up-to-date photographs as soon as possible. These were to be forthcoming, and by using the speed of the Canberra aircraft, photographs taken were processed and issued back to the unit concerned in the minimum time possible; as a result, photographic reconnaissance became a weapon of even greater significance than it had been in the Malayan Emergency.

Having established a highly efficient organisation in the Borneo territories, HQ FEAF's attention had to switch suddenly to the defence of the mainland, West Malaysia, when in the summer of 1964 the Indonesians dropped their parachutists in the Labis area. Although only three C-130s escaped the radar net, the fact that there was a gap in it caused great concern and all available fighter aircraft were put on the alert — Javelins from No 60 Squadron, Hunters from No 20 Squadron and RAAF Sabres based at Butterworth near Penang. A few days later, when the men from the 10th Gurkhas were clearing up the pockets of parachutists in the jungles near Labis, Hunters from No 20 Squadron were used to strike against the intruders, firing their rockets at discarded Indonesian parachutes in the jungle as aiming points because no other living targets were visible. When a captured Indonesian officer, thoroughly disillusioned with the way the operation had been planned and executed by his country, consented to make a full statement to that effect, his message was printed as a leaflet and a million copies were dropped by Hastings and Argosy aircraft at various places over Indonesian Kalimantan territory.

As a result of the Labis incursion, the air defence of Singapore and the mainland of Malaya was looked at most carefully and urgent steps were taken to fill the gaps in the radar cover. A 'County' class cruiser, HMS *Kent*, steamed to the Malacca Straits in an air defence role while Royal Naval Gannets from HMS *Victorious* supported the RAF coastal aircraft in maritime patrols. Other steps were taken which included eight Javelins being flown into Tengah from No 64 Squadron in the UK, welcome reinforcements to No 60 Squadron as that Squadron had already committed detachments on a semi-permanent basis in the Borneo territories. In addition, light anti-aircraft guns from the Royal Artillery moved from BAOR to Singapore where they were manned by the RAF Regiment in defence of the airfields. Finally, one missile from No 65 (SAM) Squadron, Bloodhound 11, was activated to defend Singapore Island, and to make assurance doubly sure, the deterrent was strengthened when Victor bombers from No 57 Squadron Bomber Command, based in the UK, were held over at RAF Tengah in order to show the Indonesians that Great Britain meant business.

All that remained was to make sure that the formidable array of aircraft and weapons was co-ordinated into a well-knit plan and to this end, at the end of October 1964, a full-scale air defence exercise was held in Singapore which served to boost the morale of the local people as well as serving notice on Sukarno not to attempt anything in the way of ambitious incursions. Notwithstanding this exercise, at the end of March in the following year Indonesian anti-aircraft guns, located on the Riau Islands, began firing at civilian and military aircraft leaving from or returning to the airfields in Singapore. This warlike gesture led to a rapid deterioration in relations between Indonesia and Australia because it meant that even more flying hours had to be expended in order to avoid the hostile guns: Australia's reaction was to despatch a battalion of the Royal Australian Army together with a squadron from its SAS to the Borneo territories where they were to play a full part in blunting Sukarno's aggression.

In spite of these measures, occasional incursions continued to be made by Indonesian aircraft but records show that there was only one meeting and a chance one at that, when a Javelin fighter passed an Indonesian C-130 Hercules near the border; the British pilot reported that the amazed consternation on the faces of the crew was noticeable even when the planes flashed past each other at speed. Well before the end of the Confrontation the ground forces were in a position to meet and defeat the TNI whenever they came into contact, and before the 'Claret' raids crossed into Indonesian territory the soldiers knew that they were assured of maximum support up to the boundary. Thereafter, for political reasons, there could be no air support while they operated on the Kalimantan side of the border, something that was understood, even if it made each raid hazardous and nerve-wracking in the minds of those participating — the evacuation of casualties being the biggest fear.

There were important lessons in the use of air power during the Borneo Confrontation. The Joint Headquarters worked extremely well under the one Director of Operations, Gen Walker, and then under his relief, Gen Lea. At the beginning when there were few helicopters and the Indonesians retained the initiative, there were one or two occasions when helicopters were put under direct command of a unit and this worked well. However, as the numbers built up, the more conventional centralised tasking fitted the theatre requirement well because it meant that, with their specialist knowledge, the 'taskers' used the available planes and pilots to their maximum capability as well as watching the serviceability of each aircraft, a vital factor under those climatic conditions.

It was very much a helicopter war and all three Services contributed to the full, ensuring that the machines played a dominant role in the campaign both tactically and logistically. The high serviceability rate of the aircraft was a credit to the maintenance crews who worked long hours under hot, humid conditions to ensure the maximum number of planes was available on any given day.

Finally, it was a strange war as far as the opposing air forces were concerned. Although through sheer weight of numbers the RAF's opponents in the Indonesian Air Force should have been capable of exerting an important influence on the campaign, a deep fear of retaliation from the Royal Air Force grounded it for most of the time. In addition, the Indonesian Air Force, due to chronic maintenance problems as well as indifferent administration, did not use its machines to the best advantage in support of the TNI, especially when units were in isolated camps near the international border. For the Royal Air Force, it was a most unusual campaign in which the main oppponents were the inhospitable terrain and a climate which could worsen dramatically without any warning — and not the Indonesian pilots. That there were no casualties from enemy air action is a firm indication of how Sukarno's pilots regarded their British, Australian, New Zealand and Malaysian opponents, and this fear meant that unchallenged air superiority gave immense strategic and tactical advantages to the Security Forces during all phases of the campaign. One disadvantage the RAF faced was that even when there were known Indonesian bases, established sometimes a matter of yards on the other side of the border, these retained an inviolability because for political reasons the pilots were not allowed to carry out any interdiction of camps or supply routes, however obvious those targets were to everyone who flew along the border. It must have been frustrating but in their forbearance lay the seeds of final victory because the Confrontation never escalated into a full-scale war.

Left:
One that crashed: the Wessex helicopter in which the author was travelling. He had to have his right arm amputated during an emergency jungle operation without anaesthetic.
FAA Museum

Below:
An RAF Victor bomber from No 57 Squadron Bomber Command, based in the UK, banking over Singapore. *MoD*

16 The Royal Navy Protects Malaysia

When the Brunei Revolt broke out, the initial British military response was not very urgent chiefly because the widespread nature of the uprising was not anticipated at first. Once the extent of the emergency had become apparent, the spearhead units, the 1/2nd Gurkhas followed by the Queen's Own Highlanders, were moved from Singapore by air. Then it became the task of the Royal Navy to continue the rapid build-up of troops, armoured cars, Auster aircraft and other weapons of war and this it did by using all available ships to the maximum capacity. HMS *Bulwark*, Britain's first Commando ship, with 42 Royal Marine Commando on board, acted as a fast ferry during this phase as well as operating and maintaining the helicopter force so badly needed at a crucial time. In addition, the 6th Minesweeping Squadron carried out yeoman service by supporting the land forces in a variety of ways. For example, for the assault carried out by 42 Commando against Limbang, the civilian craft used were manned by officers and men from HMS *Fiskerton* and HMS *Chorlton*. Prior to sailing, frantic repairs and servicing had to be carried out during the daylight hours before the craft chugged up river for the Marines' dawn assault on the town of Limbang.

HMS *Albion* and her sister-ship *Bulwark* had been light aircraft carriers transformed into warships of an entirely new concept: the Commando ship. In place of fixed-wing aircraft, each ship carried two squadrons of troop-carrying helicopters, a flotilla of assault landing craft and one or two Commandos of Royal Marines. Initially, and while operations were confined to the small state of Brunei, support for the land forces could be given directly from HMS *Albion*, and later HMS *Bulwark* when she arrived. However, when operations were in progress a hundred miles from the sea, it was far too far inland for the Wessex and Whirlwind helicopters to operate from the ships. The helicopters had to be based ashore leaving the Commando ship free to become an ideal ferry for vehicles, heavy equipment and troops from Singapore — not a role sought by her crew but one which was to become increasingly important as the campaign continued.

HMS *Bulwark* had already served three years in the Far East and was due to return to the UK, so that a signal was sent to HMS *Albion* to move to the Borneo waters at full speed. Her arrival was at a most opportune moment and although originally it had been intended that she would disembark 40 Royal Marine Commando at Miri, she was diverted to Kuching, the capital of Sarawak, in a move to pre-empt trouble among the CCO. To prevent any internal security problem posed by the CCO, a battery of the Royal Artillery without its guns was flown to Kuching from the ship and two days later it was reinforced by most of 40 Commando. HMS *Albion* then steamed eastward to land the remaining Commando company near Seria and to disembark one of her two helicopter squadrons at Brunei Town. The arrival of the helicopters of 846 Squadron, now ashore, and the presence of the Wessex helicopters of 845 Squadron added a new dimension to operations: no longer was it necessary to make dangerous assault landings from the air as the Queen's Own Highlanders had done earlier in the rebellion, or attempt to move in trucks along roads like 'C' Company 1/2nd Gurkhas Rifles had done in their abortive attempt to reach Seria.

HMS *Albion* was a real work horse throughout the Confrontation, a statement that can be illustrated by the fact that 12 months later the ship was to make her 15th appearance off the North Borneo coast, this time bringing squadrons of RAF Whirlwinds and Belvederes from the Middle East. The arrival of these helicopters enabled the Whirlwinds of 846 Squadron and some Wessex helicopters from 845 Squadron to rejoin HMS *Albion*, both squadrons having been based ashore since August 1963. During those 12 months the two squadrons had completed over 8,000 operational sorties.

At one stage in the Borneo Confrontation there was a force of some 16 ships operating in the waters around Borneo, most of them coming from 6 Minesweeping Squadron, with their task being to

Right:
Marines of 42 Commando RM embarking in landing craft whilst on board HMS *Bulwark*. *RM Museum*

Below:
HMS *Bulwark* about to sail from Singapore with an unusual deck park. *Author/HMS Bulwark*

Above:
The forward base of 845 Royal Naval Helicopter Squadron for its helicopters at Nanga Ghat, well over a hundred miles from their ship, HMS *Albion.*
FAA Museum

Right:
Lt Cdr G. J. 'Tank' Sherman receives the Boyd Trophy for outstanding operational service in the Borneo Territories — on behalf of his squadron, 845 RNAS. *FAA Museum*

Above:
HMS *Puncheston*, one of the coastal minesweepers that did yeoman service on a variety of tasks, especially up the larger rivers. *FAA Museum*

Below:
Naval Party 'Kilo' on patrol in a converted stores tender. These patrols stopped gun-running and gathered local intelligence. *IWM*

Right:
Arrested Indonesian gun-runners being guarded by a Naval rating from HMS *Ajax*. *IWM*

hunt, stop and search small boat traffic. Indeed, the most dangerous threat from the sea was the humble motor boat, small and powered by a quiet outboard engine. It was by such a means that arms could reach the CCO in Sarawak and the indigenous Indonesians living in North Borneo especially around the Tawau area. Ideally, fast motor torpedo-boats and gunboats would have been best suited to counter this threat but these had been scrapped in the Royal Navy, being replaced by a fleet of small coastal and inshore minesweepers specially designed to meet what was considered to be the main threat, Russian minelaying around the British Isles and in other vital sea arteries. These minesweepers were slow, undergunned and their thin wooden hulls stood high out of the water. Nevertheless they played an important role ferrying men, stores and equipment up the large rivers as well as into the coastal ports. It was a series of these mundane trips that prompted an irate officer from one of the minesweepers to say:

'We sometimes think the Army imagine that we exist to transport them. I suppose from a soldier's outlook this is understandable and they are quite right in thinking we are the only safe, effective and fast means of moving sizeable bodies of troops operationally in Borneo!'.

The minesweepers were carrying about 200 troops at a time and were particularly useful in the Third Division of Sarawak where the giant River Rejang was navigable right up to and beyond the capital Sibu, whereas there were no roads connecting Sibu with the coast or further into the interior.

Important though such roles were, it must be stressed that the Royal Navy's primary task during Confrontation was to guard the West Malaysian coastline against incursion by groups of Indonesian regulars, saboteurs and terrorists. Such a task was complicated by the swarms of fishermen and the traditional barter trade which had been carried out over the centuries between the Indonesian islands, the mainland of Malaya and Singapore. During the peak period of Confrontation Naval ships were on patrol continuously for over 700 days and nights and intercepted 90% of the known attempts to infiltrate into West Malaysia by sea. Inevitably, the brunt of the patrols was borne by the small ships of the inshore flotilla which were averaging 21 days a month at sea. It was boring and exacting work and there were few moments of excitement. Two incidents out of the normal humdrum patrolling occurred in 1965 when, first, three coastal minesweepers intercepted and caught three armed 'sampans' and during the firefight eight Indonesian soldiers were killed and 19 captured, all of whom had been trying to get into Southeast Johore. The second occurred on the other side of the water when HMS *Puncheston* stopped and searched a local boat which was carrying a huge quantiity of arms and ammunition destined for the CCO.

Unpublicised was a strange but most efficient force called Naval Party 'Kilo' which sailed hither and thither along Sarawak's South China Sea coast, seeking to prevent any infiltration by Indonesians. This force's patrol boats were camouflaged to look like local fishing boats (kotaks) and after the experiment proved successful, other naval stores tenders and landing craft were camouflaged and converted for the same role. On most ships there was a crew of four with a hidden machine gun nest. As part of their mission, these little ships sailed into coastal kampongs and up the adjoining rivers so that, in due course, the sailors became very friendly with the local Malays and Sea Dyaks in the longhouses. Apart from serving as a deterrent to hostile small boats, they were able to glean information by using the eyes and ears of the friendly fishermen.

As the military threat to East Malaysia diminished towards the end of the Confrontation, so were the Security Forces able to take opportunities to help the local people in numerous ways. The Royal Navy was not backward in helping the civilians, particularly in the Tawau area where small parties of sailors from patrolling minesweepers dispensed medical aid as well as sponsoring and organising building projects: a wide variety of projects were also undertaken by frigates or destroyers based at Tawau. Away from the coastal plain the helicopters from 845 Squadron flew in nearly 100 cholera patients from a group of longhouses to the nearest civilian hospital, and on more than one occasion lifted desperately ill people from outlying longhouses on their errand of mercy. Not surprisingly, the tribes living in the interior were sorry when the Confrontation ended because it meant that the British and Commonwealth soldiers were about to leave Borneo for the last time. The Muruts, Dyaks and other tribes living alongside the rivers were intensely pro-British and the material help that was given these primitive people during the Confrontation was something that they had never received before. With some reason they viewed their new Malaysian masters with more than a little suspicion and it was to take some time before friendly relations were established in the most inaccessible of areas.

That the effective use of British sea power played a big part in preventing the Confrontation from being escalated to an all-out war cannot be disputed. Apart from raids by a few small parties, the mainland of West Malaysia remained inviolate because Sukarno did not dare risk large parties on forays which — he soon learnt — would have ended in disaster. In the Borneo waters the Royal Navy exerted pressure quietly and efficiently so

Above:
PO Hazel of 845 Royal Naval Squadron attends sick civilians on their way to hospital. Helicopters were used on many such missions of mercy.
FAA Museum

Left:
The Penghulu (headman) of Bario presents the Captain of HMS *Albion* with some feathers in his hat — in gratitude for the help given to his village by the Royal Naval helicopters. *IWM*

that help from outside for the CCO and the indigenous Indonesians was minimal, brought to a lower pitch by constant vigilance. The land forces saw the Whirlwind and Wessex helicopters from 845 and 846 Squadrons and naturally, in their eyes, those machines were the most important part of the Royal Navy's effort. The pilots, air crew and even ground staff were in the thick of it, often operating from bases well inside the interior of Sarawak. Equally important, even though quite unspectacular, were the ships that kept the land forces supplied with the heavier sinews of war as well as rotating units to and from Singapore. The presence of the Commando ships, the minesweepers and assorted small craft meant that between 1963 and 1966 Britannia did rule the waves around the Borneo territories. The two Directors of Operations, Gen Walter Walker, and his successor Gen George Lea, were both to receive excellent support from the Royal Navy throughout the campaign with its members operating on land, sea and in the air.

Left:
Hovercraft trials on the River Rejang in the Third Division of Sarawak. The Confrontation ended before these could be properly evaluated but their noise was a problem. *AAC*

Below left:
A Wessex helicopter from the Royal Navy in a small clearing near Balaga. Pilots had to be prepared to land almost anywhere. *FAA Museum*

17 The Front Was Everywhere

On 13/14 February 1966 an incursion took place in the Tebedu area of First Division when a mixed party of Chinese IBTs and TNI crossed the border into Sarawak. A day later the party was sighted by a Border Scout, following which a camp and tracks were found in the jungle west of the Tebedu road. Next day there were a series of contacts between the Security Forces and the Indonesians during which two of the invaders were killed, with the Security Forces losing one killed and six wounded. Then, as the intelligence summary was to say, 'It appears that the enemy are splitting into small parties and a full-scale search and destroy operation is in progress'. The operation was to be called 'Mixed Bag' and it was to be one in which the Army Air Corps aircraft, in particular, played a major part.

During 'Mixed Bag' the front was nowhere yet the front was everywhere, and the insurgents had no fixed line of withdrawal: they knew that once discovered they were fighting for their lives — they were fully committed to death or survival. The operation ranged over an area of about 10 by 40 miles running northeast from Tebedu where the ground was pock-marked by small hills, covered by dense secondary jungle broken in places by open paddy-fields which had been cultivated along the bottom of the main valleys. Because of the dense nature of the country it was almost impossible to call down air strikes or even artillery fire and, on some occasions, it was difficult to be sure whether a noise, barely a few feet away, was being caused by friend or foe. On the ground, six rifle companies and a company of the Police Frontier Force were deployed in an area where visual control was impracticable and map reading a nightmare. For such a reason the CO 2/7 Gurkha Rifles, who was in command of the ground forces, spent 82 hours in a Sioux helicopter during the three weeks of the operation, using it as a command vehicle and OP (observation post) from which to conduct the battle. For the most intensive 10 days of the action, the colonel was to spend 52 hours in the air and a relay of pilots had to be provided to keep him aloft.

It was unfortunate that 'Mixed Bag' coincided with a serious defect on the Sioux as a result of which for the first four days of the operation only one of those machines was available in the whole West Brigade area. The more powerful Scout fared slightly better in serviceability terms but it was not really acceptable as a command post because of the limitations imposed by its VHF (FM) radio. However, on 7 March, Scouts were used in a variety of roles: as mobile combat command posts, as pathfinders for the RAF Whirlwinds and, at a crucial moment when speed was vital, to provide an immediate tactical lift of Gurkha troops into the thick of the battle area.

It became clear that the strength of the incursion group was between 40 and 80, some 20 of whom were known to be Indonesian paratroopers. Like many of their predecessors who had crossed the border they had expected to receive help from some of the local inhabitants, assistance in obtaining supplies and information, and as this was not to be forthcoming, any chance of gaining a worthwhile success dwindled dramatically.

It would take too long to give a day-by-day account of this extraordinary operation which entailed vigorous patrolling on the ground supported by the maximum use of air power — in the main from the Army Air Corps — to harass and harry the insurgents even after they had split up into small parties. Most of the insurgents eventually disappeared across the border in haste and confusion, leaving behind six dead bodies as well as discarded equipment, clothing and even arms to show how they had abandoned their foray into Sarawak. That more bodies were not found can be explained by the fact that the area of operations was extensive, superposed over some thousands of square miles of jungle. The 600 'searchers' could but cover a fraction of such an area and perforce they relied on tangible signs of movement to show them that the invaders had moved along a particular track in their bid to escape death or captivity.

The operation was a personal success for Lt Col Rooney who had a real 'Mixed Bag' under his command, with his sub-units operating over a wide

Right:
Operation 'Mixed Bag', February/ March 1966.

Left:
A Scout helicopter from 14 Flight Army Air Corps lands on a specially constructed bamboo platform. This helicopter was used for a variety of operational and supply tasks throughout the campaign. *AAC*

Below:
Capt Robin Adshead 6GR, attached Army Air Corps, and his Sioux helicopter. These small machines were used for a multitude of purposes including reconnaissance, liaison and communications. *IWM*

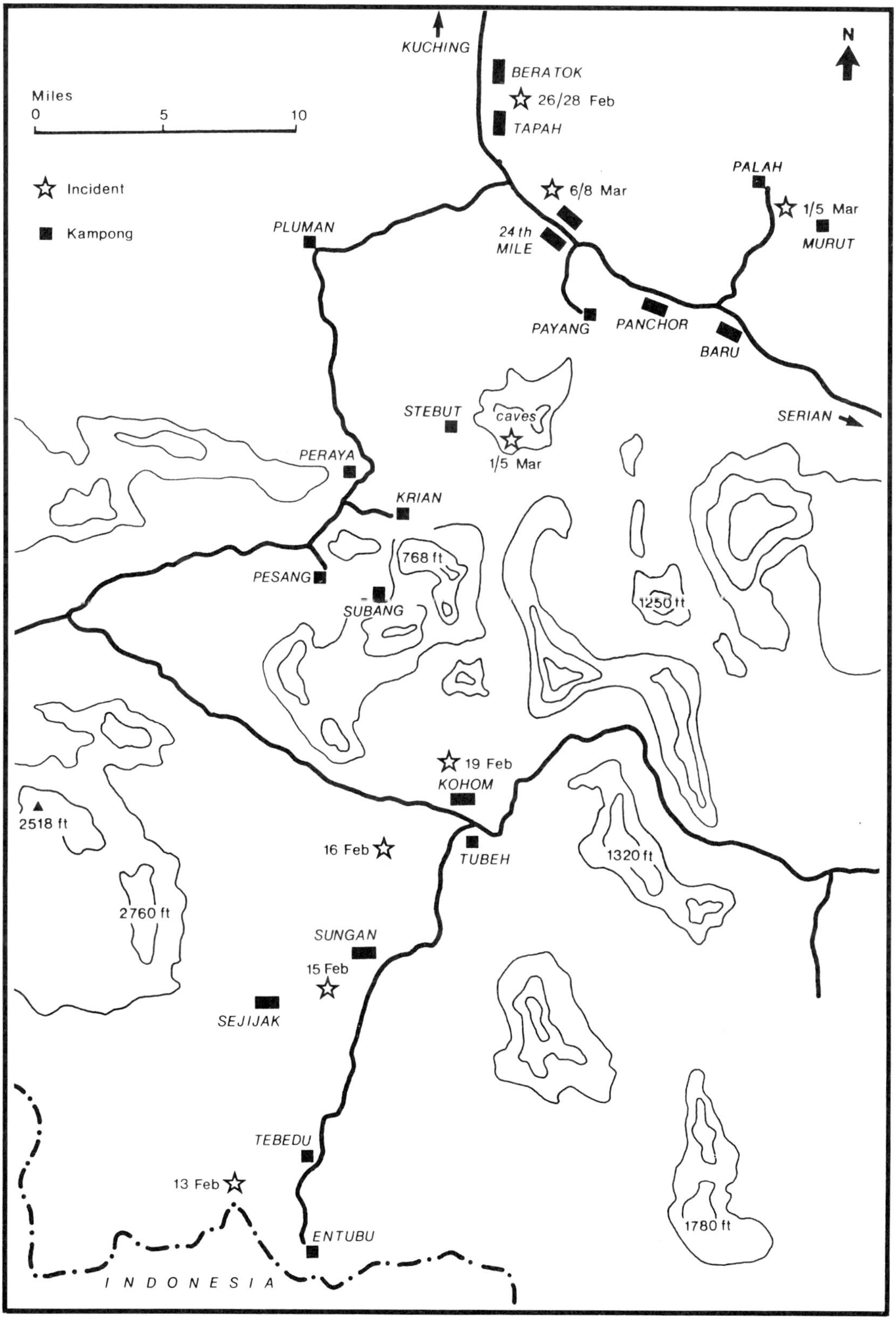
KUCHING
N
BERATOK
26/28 Feb
TAPAH
Miles
0
5
10
Incident
Kampong
PALAH
6/8 Mar
1/5 Mar
MURUT
PLUMAN
24th
MILE
PAYANG
PANCHOR
BARU
STEBUT
caves
1/5 Mar
SERIAN
PERAYA
KRIAN
768 ft
PESANG
SUBANG
1250 ft
19 Feb
KOHOM
2518 ft
16 Feb
TUBEH
1320 ft
2760 ft
SUNGAN
15 Feb
SEJIJAK
TEBEDU
13 Feb
ENTUBU
1780 ft
INDONESIA

field and having to be switched from one point to another in an attempt to stop the Indonesians from returning to a safe sanctuary in Kalimantan. It is certain that he could not have commanded or exercised control effectively without his air command post. Apart from being able to contact patrols and sub-units by radio, he was able to land when conditions so permitted and brief the commanders concerned in person. On certain occasions the colonel had to get out of the aircraft while it was still at 'the hover', a manoeuvre that had been well rehearsed before in a safe area and one that only a fit man could achieve with dexterity. It is not surprising that he was in full agreement with the commander of West Brigade, when the latter remarked: 'I command my brigade with a Scout Helicopter. I cannot do it any other way. There is no other way'. (Brig W. W. Cheyne DSO).

Although the ground forces worked extremely hard during 'Mixed Bag', there is no doubt whatever that it was a joint land-air operation, one that introduced some new techniques. The Indonesians, too, appreciated that an important role was being played by the helicopters and on more than one occasion opened fire at them. At one stage when the arrival of armed RAF Whirlwinds had been delayed, Scout aircraft were loaded with Gurkhas, and in each aircraft the Bren gunner sat in the door ready to open fire should that be necessary. A little later the Whirlwinds joined in, and indeed without the extra lift provided by the RAF Belvederes and Whirlwinds the operation would have petered out in failure. Initially there were problems because the RAF pilots were not always in the local tactical picture, so that it was found necessary to put a mobile control team at Tebedu which proved to be successful as thereafter the helicopter movements were far better co-ordinated.

Other aircraft played their part in this most interesting operation including the Austers from No 20 Flight AAC which were able to provide continuous observation over the area during the daylight hours as well as acting as mobile radio relay stations, thus enabling patrols on the ground to keep in radio contact with each other, something that the nature of the terrain made impossible without an airborne relay station.

After 'Mixed Bag' was over certain lessons were evaluated in a report — which are summarised here because they apply to the whole campaign. The prime lesson was that in counter-revolutionary warfare, and especially in jungle-covered country, the helicopter is simply indispensable as a mobile observation and command post and as a means of producing mobility for the ground forces. The report went on to say that there could never be too many helicopters. Although it was considered arming the helicopters with a suitable offensive weapon during 'Mixed Bag', it was not done and it was felt that it should never be done at the expense of the tactical lift capability. If it was necessary for a particular phase only, then it would have to be a button-on or pick-up-and-carry type of weapon.

In spite of fulsome praise for the helicopter, the report also stressed that there would have to be fixed-wing light aircraft to provide continuous surveillance of the battlefield at a relatively low cost. Although undoubtedly overshadowed by the more dramatic roles played by the helicopters, the reliable Austers enacted a major part in the operation, flying for long hours at economical flying cost. In addition, irrespective of the type of aircraft, it was considered vital that a radio be installed to provide accurate and easy communications between the ground forces and the pilot or commander in the plane. The difficult question of how the ground force commander exercises control when aircraft provided by another Service are operating in his area is one that is still discussed to this very day. If this was to be effective, the report continued, then all aircraft that had to operate at a low level air space would have to be fitted with a VHF Radio so that they could keep it in contact with the ground forces rather than adding yet another burden for the soldier to carry in the shape of a special radio set. Finally, the report ended by saying that in counter-revolutionary warfare all airmen — irrespective of their Service — had to be trained to think like the soldiers so that they could give them maximum tactical support in any operation. Although 'Mixed Bag' did not produce a large number of enemy casualties, it was to provide much food for thought by the Joint Land-Air Warfare Staffs and helped them to evolve new doctrines for the future.

18 Peace with Honour — and the Lessons

In March 1965 when Maj Gen Walter Walker handed over to his successor, Maj Gen George Lea, he exhorted his forces to even greater efforts saying: 'Do not slacken. Our best contribution to peace is to convince the Indonesians that aggression will fail, no matter in what form it may come'.

The choice of George Lea to follow Walter Walker was an inspired one. Very much a soldier's general, Lea had commanded 22 SAS during its period of greatest achievement in Malaya. Wisely Lea had let the efficient machine he inherited from Walker run itself while he mastered his intricate and difficult job. Thereafter his transparent honesty and ability to weld a diverse team together meant that the campaign in Borneo continued to be waged with maximum effect by all three Services, Commonwealth as well as British.

With the Indonesians being forced to abandon their forward positions, defeat in the long term became inevitable. The TNI's logistical and supply arrangements were primitive although its soldiers fought with gallantry on several occasions. But deprived of efficient medical or administrative support, their morale was sapped as time passed and conditions worsened. Within Indonesia itself, Sukarno's Controntasi had added considerably to the parlous economic problems which crippled the country and gave rise to ever-growing cries of grievances. In late September 1965, with 'The Night of the Generals' came the day of reckoning.

Unlike the popular West Irian campaign, Indonesia's opposition to Malaysia excited the hostility of world opinion and even non-aligned countries showed little or no sympathy for Sukarno. Internally the Communist Party (PKI) orchestrated the protests under its leader, Aidit. The PKI was at its zenith of influence but its leaders realised that until they won over the Army, there was no chance of them taking complete power. Therefore, the gospel of Communism was preached to junior officers and cadets in all three Services and by 1965 the PKI had established strong links with the Air Force in particular. During August 1965 Sukarno became seriously ill so that the various political groupings began plotting for the succession. PKI leader Aidit urged his Politburo to support certain 'progressive officers' who were prepared to forestall an army coup. During the night of 30 September the conspirators struck when six senior generals were either murdered in front of their families or taken away to be killed. The only one who escaped was Gen Nasution, but not before his five-year old daughter had been killed. Then matters went wrong because while the conspirators vacillated next day, decisive steps were taken by Gen Suharto and the coup was crushed within a matter of hours.

The extent of PKI involvement, or indeed that of Sukarno, in the coup is impossible to estimate. What can be said is that the Army under Gen Suharto at once seized the opportunity to crush its hated rivals, storming the PKI headquarters and then murdering well-known Communists. Despite this show of force by the TNI, Sukarno refused to ban the PKI whereupon the Army took the law into its own hands and terror raged for weeks: in Central Java alone, tens of thousands were killed, including Aidit himself. The carnage spread to East Java, Bali and other provinces and it is estimated that between 200,000 and 500,000 perished.

While Sukarno continued to rant and rave about 'Crushing Malaysia', Gen Suharto initiated secret talks with the Malaysian Government with a view to ending the costly war. Week by week Sukarno's influence dwindled and once his Foreign Minister, Subandrio, had been condemned to death and the political power of the Air Force smashed, Sukarno found himself isolated, virtually a prisoner in the gilded palace.

Peace came on 11 August 1966, a peace that brought to an end the strange undeclared war in Borneo, a war that rarely hit the headlines because for a variety of reasons both sides shunned publicity. The stamina and health of the British, Gurkha and Commonwealth soldiers had withstood the stress and rigours of operating for long periods in some of the toughest terrain in the world. Their determination and physical fitness

Right:
Lt-Col George Lea, Commanding Officer 22 SAS (later to become Major General and Director of Operations, Borneo 1965/66). *SAS Association*

Below:
HRH Prince Philip paid a visit to the Borneo Territories in 1965. Here he is talking to personnel from 11 Flight Army Air Corps. *AAC*

inspired a flood of congratulatory messages that poured in after the Confrontation was over. Many came from the local people who had feared Sukarno and his ambitions. The then Secretary of State for War, the Rt Hon Denis Healey MP, paid tribute to the soldiers of the British and Commonwealth nations:

'The campaign has been a model of inter-Service co-operation; all three Services have worked as one. We should pay tribute to all those, from the highest to the lowest rank, who have served alongside the forces of our Commonwealth partners and who have made so signal a contribution to the settlement which has been achieved. I should like to pay a special tribute to the Gurkhas'.

It was this blend which helped to keep the newly formed Malaysian state intact.

The Confrontation was a small war by most standards, and by those of Korea and Vietnam a very small war. At its height there were only about 17,000 Commonwealth Servicemen in Borneo with another 10,000 immediately available elsewhere in the Far East. The Commonwealth casualties for the whole period were 114 killed and 181 wounded, while the civilians suffered 36 killed, 53 wounded and four captured. Some would affirm that even these were too many but as the price of a nation's very existence against a huge adversary they were slight, so slight as to be scarcely credible. Moreover, victory was total both in the military and political sense and was not the sort in which the enemy was ground to pulp and smashed into submission; it was the better kind that all wars ought to aim for but few achieve, whereby the objectives are limited to those that are truly vital, the force used is adequate to ensure success, de-escalation is pursued whenever possible, and the inevitable war of words is based as far as possible on truth. In such a case when the day is won and the least physical and mental damage has been caused, friendship can be renewed with few hard feelings. The vital achievement was Malaysia's complete independence of Indonesia — even to the extent of voluntarily retaining British bases on its territory, which it chose to do after the conflict was over. And in a remarkably quick time friendship was revived between Indonesia on the one hand and Malaysia and Great Britain and their Commonwealth partners on the other.

Sukarno tried to dominate the tip of Asia and its islands and establish Maphilindo, to revive Indonesia's ancient empire. He tried to do it tactically by armed subversion and infiltration, hoping to establish cells of terrorists and saboteurs from which he could build up internal support, and then by aggression from over the border threaten the whole nation of Malaysia. Unlike the Malayan Emergency, therefore, it was not just an internal security campaign, and the dual threat posed by the TNI and the 'volunteers' in their camps along the border, together with the CCO within Sarawak itself, was real and dangerous. These threats were beaten by prompt reaction and by inflicting disproportionate casualties until Indonesia was convinced that its aim of crushing Malaysia was unattainable. What were these 'disproportionate casualties' that proved so decisive? At least 590 killed and 22 wounded for certain, but the number must be increased by those who could not be counted, especially the victims of the cross-border raids, added to which were 771 captured of whom not a single man was tortured or murdered while in captivity. It could be said that the 'Claret' operations actually saved Indonesian lives because they were launched to pre-empt and to deter the TNI from crossing the border on incursions which invariably were extremely costly when they did so.

The victory was first and foremost a military one. It is true that the parlous Indonesian economy tempted the new regime under Suharto to seek peace in 1966; that undoubtedly was an important factor. The significance of the military contribution can best be judged by asking what would have happened if Great Britain and its Commonwealth partners had not given it. There can be no doubt that Borneo certainly, and the mainland of Malaya possibly, would have come under the complete control of the Indonesians. Indonesia sought a solution by force and had to be convinced by force that it could not succeed — as Suharto was by 1966 — and only then was a political settlement possible. The hundreds of small contacts in widely dispersed jungle areas had as much and as direct an effect on the political outcome as did the massive carnage in other larger wars. The actions demonstrated the political will to keep Malaysia intact. Borneo could so easily have become another Vietnam and it is against this background that its success must be measured. Only leadership of a very high quality, first by Gen Walter Walker and then by Gen George Lea, and troops of a very high standard of training and versatility, prevented the conflict from escalation into a full-scale war.

The war did in fact turn a full circle from mere encounters with small parties of terrorists to conventional warfare at battalion level but it never reached the degree of total war. Air power was used to maximum effect without ever unleashing its full potential either by bombing or strafing, while strict instructions ensured that the Royal Air Force never took any offensive action against targets where there were known civilian habitations or against any base or camp on the Kalimantan side of the border. Likewise, the Royal Navy acted as a powerful deterrent by warning off any incursion by sea and preventing gun running which

Right:
An Auster which crashed from 7 Flight Army Air Corps. The passenger (an Army Padre) was killed. *AAC*

Below:
Two Indonesian prisoners being taken into custody at Sibu, capital of Third Division of Sarawak. *AAC*

could have brought in the weapons of war which were badly needed by the CCO in the urban areas. Without weapons or ammunition the CCO was unable to pose any dangerous threat internally.

At the onset in 1963 and 1964 the Security Forces were fighting terrorists, but by the time Gen Walker handed over to Gen Lea in 1965, they were involved in actions against well-equipped, highly trained regular troops, supported by artillery and mortars. It was a bitter attempt by the Indonesians to build up a series of attacks which reached a level of that achieved in the Burma campaign against the Japanese. During the final stages Lea, the new Director of Operations, was commanding forces operating at a much higher level of insurgency warfare which not only involved high standards of patrolling and battlecraft but the fullest use of artillery and mortars, with air offensive always near at hand should an emergency dictate its use.

The overall strategy adopted by the Malaysian and British Governments, and put into effect by the two Directors of Operations, was completely vindicated by the result, which Denis Healey described as follows: 'In the history books it will be recorded as one of the most efficient uses of military force in the history of the world'.

So much for the strategy, now a quick look at the tactics adopted, particularly those used by the ground forces. With so many possible incursion routes to watch, the vital importance of a surveillance screen was appreciated and the decision to use local people, based on their own kampongs and longhouses, to act as 'eyes and ears', meant that a most constructive step had been taken along the path to victory. Fortunately, too, the Borneo tribes were for the most part pro-British and had never looked on their old colonial masters with anything but affection. If at the onset there were those who wavered or sat on the fence, the murder of the Border Scouts in Long Jawi — apart from being a criminal act — was totally counter-productive to Indonesia's cause.

Like Templer in Malaya, Gen Walker fully appreciated the importance of early, accurate information, so that another important cog had to be reliable, widespread communications. The four-man patrols of the SAS, with their long-range sets, were well equipped for such a role, but more was needed, and in time VHF re-broadcast facilities were extended to cover the whole area of operations. This was achieved by setting up re-broadcast stations on two or three of the highest peaks in West Sarawak where small detachments carried out a two-week tour of duty, often living in the clouds from day to day, and reliant on helicopters to bring in food, equipment and, on the due date, relief signallers to take over the most important duty. (Two weeks was considered to be the maximum in such solitude.) As a consequence the VHF Command Net, incorporating air and ground units, worked most effectively by day and night, thus enabling the swift transit of operational information to be passed as a result of which reaction time was cut down to the bare minimum.

The key to quick reaction was, of course, the helicopters which provided the battalions with the necessary degree of speed, mobility and flexibility. Over and over again did they prove themselves to be the real battle-winners, and an astute battalion commander with a few 'choppers' could and did block the guerillas at every turn so that they were under the impression that an entire army was on their heels. Mention has also been made of the increased flexibility given to the fire plan when 105mm howitzers and heavy mortars were moved from one company base to another, thus giving the Indonesians an overwhelming impression of strength all along the border area.

Beneath their jungle canopy, those troops who already had lived and fought in the jungles of Malaya proved invaluable at a time when the majority of the British infantrymen — through no fault of their own — had little or no experience of jungle operations and, by dint of concentrated training and bitter experience, had to relearn the techniques that had been perfected in the Burma campaign. By having to remain in the jungle for so long, and especially on 'Claret' raids over the border into Kalimantan which often involved several days without air drops, the soldiers participating bitterly regretted the heavy loads they were forced to carry. Weapons such as the SLR and GPMG were heavy and unwieldy, wireless sets were cumbersome, and rations in their packs were unsuitable and bulky for the climate, terrain and role the infantrymen had to play. The plea for lightweight equipment, radios and rations was one that did not meet with a quick response by Whitehall which failed to appreciate that victory in guerilla warfare goes to the tougher, more resourceful soldier, one who can remain for longer periods at peak physical condition in the jungle — which means that the load he has to carry on his back must be cut down to the minimum. An important lesson this, and one that was only resolved in the late autumn of the campaign.

It is difficult to resist drawing comparisons with Vietnam where an over-sophisticated American army, and an air force which dropped four times more bombs than it had in the whole of World War 2, failed to win a limited guerilla war against a puny nation. They were outfought and outwitted: the United States poured into the Vietnam war eight years of effort, the lives of 50,000 young men, the good health of another 300,000, $150billion of its hard-earned tax money, and the honour and prestige of their nation, especially in the Far

Below:

An Iban tribeswoman demonstrates a dance to men of a patrol. Winning the confidence of the local people played an important part in the overall strategy. *IWM*

Below:

A patrol of the 1st Battalion Irish Guards build its 'Basha' for the night. All men had to learn to live in the jungle and make themselves as comfortable as possible under trying conditions. *IWM*

Above:

Walker's sixth principle. A medical orderly from the Green Jackets opens his 'surgery' in a longhouse and helps to win over the local people to the Government's cause. *IWM*

East. America fought a costly no-win war which left South-East Asia in a far worse condition that it was before American intervention began. But perhaps it could have been won if the strategy adopted from the beginning had been based on the one adopted by Great Britain and Malaya in both the Emergency and Confrontation? It must be remembered that in both Malaya and Borneo the enemy was at least as formidable as the Viet Cong had been in the early 1960s while Indonesia was just as strong militarily as North Vietnam. If either campaign had been mismanaged, then this country and her Commonwealth partners could well have been drawn into an ever-escalating war which would have ended in disaster.

The Borneo campaign stands out as being a notable example of how highly trained professional infantrymen, with full support from the other arms and services, can achieve a decisive victory against a well-armed and aggressive foe. There was little destruction of the countryside and little disruption of the normal life of the civilian population so that when the Confrontation ended in 1966, reversion to peacetime conditions was virtually automatic and painless. There had been no aerial bombing, no interdiction, no napalm or large scale defoliation of the jungle: indeed, during the whole campaign not a single bomb was dropped nor a rocket fired near any longhouse or known civilian habitation.

The Security Forces mastered the difficult physical conditions and secured the willing help of the inhabitants. They learnt, too, to cope with the most difficult terrain and in this connection mention must be made of the fact that prior to the Borneo Confrontation, the majority of Gurkha soldiers could not swim. Hailing from a landlocked country, there had been little opportunity or necessity for them to learn but, after losing several soldiers in the fast-flowing rivers of Borneo, the whole Brigade of Gurkhas put swimming training as a priority until nearly every man mastered the art. Such a lesson has not been forgotten in peacetime.

When we cast our minds back to Gen Walker's arrival in Brunei and recall the five points that he jotted down before taking over as Director of Operations, it is clear that those principles were all lessons that he, and others, had learnt during the Malayan Emergency. Those five points were the 'props' on which he built the early stages of the campaign: the Joint Headquarters; day to day co-ordination of civilian, police and military authorities; the timely and accurate information involving a first-class Intelligence machine; the speed, mobility and flexibility of the Security Forces, using in particular the helicopters and Pioneer aircraft; and finally, domination of the jungle by highly trained professional infantryman who could rely on immediate support from the air. Those were important lessons from the Emergency and by the time the Confrontation had ended all had increased in significance. Fortunate it was that the British had been through such a long rehearsal before Sukarno began his aggressive acts against the nearly formed state of Malaysia. Walker's sixth principle — which he later added — was one that he had seen Field Marshal Templer using to good effect, winning the people over to the Government's cause.

In general terms, Sukarno was beaten because the Security Forces had the advantage of a major military base in the right place — Singapore; in addition, there was the advanced island base of Labuan which, although only manned by a small detachment as a staging post at the beginning, became the keystone of the air effort between 1963 and 1966. Moreover, the British and Commonwealth forces enjoyed complete command of the sea and air; little escaped the vigilance of the Naval ships and their associated small boats, and of the air crews of all three Services.

Finally, morale of all the Security Forces was so high that any visitor could positively feel it. That it was so was partly from pride and a high degree of professional skill and achievement, but also from a sense of purpose. All those who served in the Borneo territories could see that there was a job really worth doing, a job which ensured that the ordinary village dweller could choose his own way of life, poor and primitive though it might be, without living in fear of coercion or being threatened with torture or death. With the vast majority of the people firmly behind the Malaysian and Commonwealth Forces, the Indonesians faced handicaps which, in the end, meant that the long drawn-out war drained the stability and the economy of their own country.

The 'undeclared war' was in many respects an unknown one because the fighting was poorly reported and few pictures of any significance reached the television screens in the United Kingdom or elsewhere in the world. That this was so was not the fault of the war correspondents who either were not allowed to see what they wanted or tell all they had learnt during their visits. As to whether such extreme sensitivity was justified is debatable, but perhaps on balance the two Directors of Operations gained from the silence which enabled them to mount the 'Claret' cross-border raids without news-hungry journalists breathing down their necks and in a rush to 'scoop' their fellows, breaking security. In complete contrast, the Falklands War was invariably fought before the eyes and in the ears of the world so that the Government and senior Service officers were constantly seeking to tread a difficult path to ensure the necessary security for operational reasons while satisfying the desire by everyone in the UK to know what was going on. Although the 'undeclared war' never hit the headlines, certainly it was a campaign that 'witnessed one of the most efficient uses of military force in the history of the world'.

Above:
A block and pulley system used to transfer a 105mm howitzer across a river. Improvisation solved many problems. *IWM*

Appendices

1 UK and Commonwealth Serving Units

Military units which served in the Malayan Emergency
16 June 1948-31 July 1960

Note: It is not practicable to record detailed dates as several units carried out more than one tour as well as moving in and out of the theatre of operations during a tour.

United Kingdom
1st King's Dragoon Guards
4th Queen's Own Hussars
11th Hussars (Prince Albert's Own)
12th Royal Lancers (Prince of Wales)
13/18th Royal Hussars (Queen Mary's Own)
15th/19th The King's Royal Hussars
2nd Field Regiment RA
25th Field Regiment RA
26th Field Regiment RA
48th Field Regiment RA
1st Singapore Regiment RA
100 Field Battery RAA
101 Field Battery RAA
105 Field Battery RAA
11 Independent Field Squadron RE
50 Gurkha Field Engineer Regiment RE
51 Field Engineer Regiment RE
74 Field Park Squadron RE
410 Independent Plant Troop RE
17th (Gurkha) Signal Regiment
208 (Commonwealth) Signal Squadron
Malaya Command Signal Squadron
3rd Grenadier Guards
2nd Coldstream Guards
2nd Scots Guards
1st Bn The Queen's Royal Regiment (West Surrey)
1st Bn The Royal Lincolnshire Regiment
1st Bn The Devonshire Regiment
1st Bn The Suffolk Regiment
1st Bn The Somerset Light Infantry (Prince Albert's)
1st Bn The West Yorkshire Regiment (The Prince of Wales Own)
1st Bn The East Yorkshire Regiment (The Duke of York's Own)
1st Bn The Green Howards (Alexandra, Prince of Wales Own Yorkshire Regiment)
1st Bn The Royal Scots Fusiliers
1st Bn The Cheshire Regiment
2nd Bn The Royal Welsh Fusiliers
1st Bn The South Wales Borderers
1st Bn The Kings Own Scottish Borderers
1st Bn The Cameronians (Scottish Rifles)
1st Bn The Royal Inniskilling Fusiliers
1st Bn The Worcestershire Regiment
1st Bn The Royal Hampshire Regiment
1st Bn The Sherwood Foresters (Nottinghamshire and Derbyshire Regiment)
1st Bn The Loyal Regiment (North Lancashire)
1st Bn 3rd East Anglian Regiment (16th/44th Foot)
1st Bn The Queen's Own Royal West Kent Regiment
1st Bn The King's Own Yorkshire Light Infantry
1st Bn The Manchester Regiment
1st Bn Seaforth Highlanders (Ross-Shire Buffs, The Duke of Albany's)
1st Bn The Gordon Highlanders
1st/2nd King Edward VII's Own Gurkha Rifles (The Sirmoor Rifles)
2nd/2nd King Edward VII's Own Gurkha Rifles
1st/6th Queen Elizabeth's Own Gurkha Rifles
2nd/6th Queen Elizabeth's Own Gurkha Rifles
1st/7th Duke of Edinburgh's Own Gurkha Rifles
2nd/7th Duke of Edinburgh's Own Gurkha Rifles
1st/10th Princess Mary's Own Gurkha Rifles
2nd/10th Princess Mary's Own Gurkha Rifles
1st Bn The Rifle Brigade (Prince Consort's Own)
22 Special Air Service Regiment
The Independent Parachute Squadron
40 Commando Royal Marines
42 Commando Royal Marines
45 Commando Royal Marines

Commonwealth
The Royal Malay Regiment (six battalions formed before end of Emergency under two Brigade headquarters with supporting arms and services)
1st Singapore Infantry Regiment
1st Bn The King's African Rifles
2nd Bn The King's African Rifles
3rd Bn The King's African Rifles
1st Bn The Northern Rhodesia Regiment
1st Bn The Fiji Infantry Regiment
1st Bn The Royal Australian Regiment
2nd Bn The Royal Australian Regiment
3rd Bn The Royal Australian Regiment
1st Bn The New Zealand Regiment
2nd Bn The New Zealand Regiment
The Rhodesia Squadron (Special Air Service)
The New Zealand Squadron (Special Air Service)

Throughout the Emergency there were units,sub units, or individuals from all the normal supporting services:

Royal Army Chaplain's Department
Royal Army Service Corps
Royal Army Medical Corps
Royal Army Ordnance Corps
Corps of Royal Electrical and Mechanical Engineers
Corps of Royal Military Police
Royal Army Pay Corps
Royal Army Educational Corps
Army Catering Corps
Queen Alexandra's Royal Army Nursing Corps

Military Units which served in the Borneo Confrontation 8 December 1962-August 1966
Note: In some cases, sub-units only moved to the Borneo Territories.

United Kingdom
The Life Guards
The Queen's Dragoon Guards
B Sqn Queen's Royal Irish Rangers
4th Royal Tank Regiment (RTR)
5th Royal Tank Regiment (RTR) (just before operations ended)
3 Locating Troop, from 3 Royal Horse Artillery
20th Medium Regiment RA (12 and 43 Btys)
40th Light Regiment (38, 129 and 137 Btys)
4th Light Regiment RA (RHQ and all btys)
45 Light Regiment RA (RHQ and all btys)
94th Locating Regiment RA
29 Commando Light Regiment (20, 79 and 145 Btys)
95 Commando Light Regiment (7, 8 and 148 Btys)
12, 16 and 22 Light Air Defence Regiments (two btys each)
6 Light Regiment (two btys and Locating Troop)
49 Field Regiment (Air OP Troop only)
Federation of Malaysian Artillery (two btys)
The Royal Engineers
Port Operating Squadron, Royal Engineers
50 Gurkha Field Engineer Regiment
The Royal Signals
The Gurkha Signals Regiment
The Scots Guards (with one company of Irish Guards under command)
The Guards Independent Parachute Company
The Royal Leicestershires
The Royal Ulster Rifles
The Queen's Own Highlanders
The Gordon Highlanders
The Argyll and Sutherland Highlanders
The Queen's Own Buffs (from mid-July 1966 only)
The King's Own Scottish Borderers
The Durham Light Infantry
The Royal Warwickshire Fusiliers (as campaign was ending)
The Royal Hampshire (from June 1966 only)
The King's Own Yorkshire Light Infantry
2nd Battalion Parachute Regiment
The Gurkha Independent Parachute Company
1/2nd Royal Green Jackets (KRRC)
1/3rd Royal Green Jackets
A, B, and D Squadrons, 22nd Special Air Services
The Army Air Corps
1/2nd and 2/2nd KEO Gurkha Rifles
1/6th and 2/6th QEO Gurkha Rifles
1/7th and 2/7th DEO Gurkha Rifles
1/10th and 2/10th PMO Gurkha Rifles
40 Commando Royal Marines
42 Commando Royal Marines
Special Boat Section Royal Marines

Commonwealth
3rd Royal Malay Regiment
5th Royal Malay Regiment
Federation Reconnaissance Regiment
Malayan Police Field Force
North Borneo Field Force
Sarawak Police Field Force
The Border Scouts
102 and 'A' Btys of the Royal Australian Artillery
3rd Battalion Royal Australian Regiment
1st Battalion Royal New Zealand Regiment
The New Zealand Squadron (Special Air Services)

Throughout the Confrontation, there were units, sub-units or individuals from all the normal supporting Services:

The Royal Corps of Transport
The Gurkha Transport Regiment
Royal Army Chaplain's Department
Royal Army Medical Corps
Royal Army Ordnance Corps
Corps of Royal Electrical and Mechanical Engineers
Corps of Royal Military Police
Royal Army Pay Corps
Royal Army Educational Corps
Army Catering Corps
Queen Alexandra's Royal Army Nursing Corps

Ships of the Royal Navy which served 'in Borneo Waters'
8 December 1962-August 1966

Commando Carriers: *Albion, Bulwark*
Minesweeper Support Ships: *Manxman, Woodbridge Haven*
Despatch Vessel: *Alert*
Destroyers: *Barrosa, Caesar, Cambrian, Carysfort, Delight, Devonshire, Kent*
Frigates: *Ajax, Blackpool, Brighton, Chichester, Dido, Euryalus, Lincoln, Llandaff, Loch Fada, Loch Killisport, Loch Lomond, Plymouth, Salisbury, Whitby, Zest*
Coastal Minesweepers: *Chawton, Dartington, Dufton, Fiskerton, Hickleton, Houghton* (note 1), *Hubberston* (note 1), *Ivermoriston, Kildarton, Lanton, Maryton, Penston, Picton, Puncheston, Santon* (note 1), *Sheraton, Thankerton, Wilkieston, Woolaston*
Royal Fleet Auxiliary: *Eddyrock, Fort Charlotte, Gold Ranger, Tideflow, Tidepool, Wave Sovereign*

Note 1: RNZN manned.
There were also ships from the Royal Australian, Royal New Zealand and Royal Malaysian Navies 'on station' at many times during the Confrontation, playing a full part in what was essentially a Commonwealth operation.

RAF Squadrons engaged during the Confrontation

Squadron	*Aircraft*	*Main Base*	*Detachments*	*Tasks*
20	Hunter GA9	Tengah	Labuan/Kuching	Air Defence Patrols
60	Javelin F9	Tengah	Labuan/Kuching	Air Defence Patrols
64	Javelin F9	Tengah	Labuan/Kuching	Air Defence Patrols
81	Canberra PR7	Tengah	Labuan	Photo/recce
34	Beverley C1	Seletar	Labuan	Supply to forward areas
215	Argosy C1	Changi	Labuan	Supply to forward areas
205	Shackleton MR2	Changi	Labuan	Maritime recce
209	Twin Pioneer CC1	Seletar	Various air strips	Supply to forward areas
66	Belvedere HC1	Seletar	Kuching	Heavy lift supply to forward areas
110	Whirlwind 10 Sycamore 14	Seletar	Various air strips	General helicopter supply
103	Whirlwind 10	UK	Various air strips	General helicopter supply
230	Whirlwind 10	UK	Various air strips	General helicopter supply
45	Canberra B15	Tengah	Labuan	Offensive standby
52	Valetta C1	Butterworth	Labuan	Medium range transport
28	Hunter GA9	Kai Tak	Labuan/Kuching	Air Defence Patrols
48	Hastings C1/2	Changi	Labuan	Medium range transport
65 (SAM)	Bloodhound	Seletar	Kuching	Air Defence

2 Order of Battle

Air Forces Order of Battle — Squadrons Available 1948-1960

Type of Support	*Type of Aircraft*	*Jun 1948*	*Sep 1949*	*Jul 1950*	*Aug 1951*	*Dec 1952*	*Dec 1953*	*Dec 1954*	*Dec 1955*	*Dec 1956*	*Dec 1957*	*Dec 1958*	*Dec 1959*	*Jul 1960*
Offensive	Single engined	1	2	2	$\frac{1}{4}$	1	1	1	3	3	2	1	2	3
	Twin engined	—	1	2	$2\frac{3}{4}$	3	2	2	1	—	1	2	3	3
	Four engined	—	—	2	1	1	2	$1\frac{1}{2}$	—	1	1	—	—	—
	Flying boat (at call)	1	1	2	$1\frac{1}{2}$	$1\frac{1}{2}$	$1\frac{1}{2}$	2	1	1	1	—	—	—
Transport	Single engined	—	—	—	—	—	—	1 Flt	1 Flt	1 Flt	1 Flt	1 Flt	1 Flt	1 Flt
	Twin engined	1	1	1	1	1	1	Detachment from FE Transport Wing equivalent to 1 Flt						
	Light helicopter	—	—	2 h/c	2 h/c	5 h/c	1	1	1	1	1	1	—	—
	Medium helicopter	—	—	—	—	—	1	2	2	1	1	1	1 Flt	1 Flt
Communications (including voice aircraft)	Various	1	1	1	1	1	1	$1\frac{1}{2}$	$1\frac{1}{2}$	$1\frac{1}{2}$	$1\frac{1}{2}$	$1\frac{1}{2}$	$1\frac{1}{2}$	$1\frac{1}{2}$
Reconnaissance	Various (PR)	1	1	1	1	1	1	1	1 (plus Bomber Command detachment)	1	1	1	1	1
	Auster (VR)	1	1	1	1	1	1	1	1	1 (plus MAAF at call)	1	1	1	1

Ground Forces Order of Battle 1948-1957

ARMY

	Jun 1948	*Jan 1949*	*Oct 1950*	*Aug 1951*	*Jun 1952*	*Jan 1953*	*Jun 1954*	*Jan 1955*	*Jan 1956*	*Jan 1957*	*Aug 1957*
Armoured Car Regiments	—	1	2	2	2	2	2	2	2	2	1
Armoured Car Squadrons	—	—	—	—	—	1	1	1	1	1	2
Field Regiments	—	—	—	—	—	—	—	—	1	1	1
Field Batteries	—	—	1	1	1	1	2	2	1	2	2
HAA Batteries	—	—	—	—	—	—	1	1	1	1	1
Field Engineer Regiments	—	—	—	—	—	—	1	2	2	2	2
Infantry Battalions	10	15	19	19	21	23	22	22	23	23	21
Commando Brigade	—	—	1	1	—	—	—	—	—	—	—
Malayan Scouts	—	—	1	1	1	—	—	—	—	—	—
22nd SAS Regiment (3 Squadrons)	—	—	—	—	—	1	1	1	1	1	1
NZ SAS Squadron	—	—	—	—	—	—	—	—	1	1	1
Squadron, The Parachute Regiment	—	—	—	—	—	—	—	—	1	1	—

POLICE

	Jun 1948	*Jan 1949*	*Jan 1950*	*Jan 1951*	*Jan 1952*	*Jan 1953*	*Jan 1954*	*Jan 1955*	*Jan 1956*	*Jan 1957*	*Aug 1957*
Regular Police	c9,000	12,767	16,220	16,814	22,187	36,737	24,427	19,659*	16,840		22,363*
Special Constabulary	—	33,610	29,987	43,475	44,878	33,570	27,208	23,238	23,238		22,409
Home Guard (average strength for year)	—	—	—	200,000	c250,000	210,000	172,500	152,000	132,000		

*Includes 2,819 and 2,915 Police Field Force

Communist Terrorist Organisation — Strength by States 1948-1960

State	*1948 (Jul)*	*1949 (Mar)*	*1950*	*1951*	*1952*	*1953*	*1954*	*1955*	*1956 (Jan)*	*1957 (Jan)*	*1957 (Dec)*	*1958 (Dec)*	*1959 (Sep)*	*1960 (Jan)*	*1960 (Jul)*	*Total Strength of MCP 1947 (Feb)*
(S Thailand)									295	304	183	485	455	495	488	
Kedah/Perlis	350	520									91	58	53	—	—	560
Penang									49	42	40	23	9	4	—	535
Kelantan	200	50							147	140	108	8	—	—	—	200
Trengganu		120							17	29	22	9	8	8	8	250
Perak	500	440	No breakdown						906	778	774	237	155	100	65	1,990
Pahang	300	230	available						139	44	42	34	20	16	3	1,920
Selangor	300	580							167	101	59	4	—	—	—	2,000
Negri Sembilan	150	210							220	117	55	2	—	—	—	795
Malacca									102	59	13	—	—	—	—	385
Jahore	500	400							524	452	294	8	4	—	—	2,990
(Singapore)	—	—							—	—	—	—	—	—	—	965
Total	2,300*	2,550*	3,923	7,292	5,765	4,373	3,402	2,798	2,566	2,066	1,681	868	704	623	564	12,590

*Estimated totals
MCP=Malayan Communist Party

Below:
HMS *Albion* — like her sister ship, HMS *Bulwark*, she spent much of her time ferrying men and valuable equipment to the Borneo Territories.
FAA Museum

3 Bibliography

Books

Noel Barber: *The War of the Running Dogs*

G. Blaxland: *The Regiment Departs*

Richard Clutterbuck: *Guerillas and Terrorists*

Peter Dickens: *SAS The Jungle Frontier*

B. Dahon: Sukarno and the Struggle for Indonesian Independence

Tony Geraghty: *'Who Dares Wins'*

M. C. A. Henniker: *Red Star over Malaya*

H. D. James and Dennis Sheil-Small: *The Undeclared War; A Pride of Gurkhas*

Air Marshal Sir David Lee: *Eastward — The History of the Far East Air Force since 1945*

A. Nasution: *Fundamentals of Guerilla Warfare*

Tom Pocock: *The Fighting General*

E. D. Smith: *East of Kathmandu; Britain's Brigade of Gurkhas*

Articles and Journals

The following have written excellent articles on either the Malayan Emergency or the Borneo Confrontation, all of which have been most useful:

Gen Sir Walter Walker KCB, CBE, DSO
Maj (now Colonel) C. J. D. Bullock OBE, MC
Lt-Col G. A. S. Truell, late Royal Artillery
Maj-Gen K. Perkins CB, MBE, DFC
Richard Sim and David Miller

In addition, I am most grateful to the Air Historical Branch for being allowed to reproduce three or four of their annexes which first appeared in their *The Malayan Emergency, 1948-1960.*

Finally, my thanks to the publishers concerned for allowing me to draw on and quote from articles written by myself which have appeared in their magazines.

Below:
A 'Voice' Dakota used for aerial propaganda broadcasts, aimed at inducing the CTs to surrender.
IWM